WHEN SUCCESS ISN'T ENOUGH

purpose is plenty

Mary Detweiler

credo
house publishers

ISBN: 978-1-62586-177-1

Cover design by Valerie Feller
Interior design by Frank Gutbrod
Editing by Donna Huisjen

Printed in the United States of America

First edition

Table of Contents

INTRODUCTION

If you were to examine my life, you may or may not see it as successful. Though my lifestyle allows me to live comfortably, I am far from wealthy. I am not powerful or famous, and I do not occupy a position of status. I am, however, committed, to the best of my ability, to live a life of purpose.

God created each one of us for a specific purpose, and he designed us to fulfill that purpose. In his book *The Purpose Driven Life*, Rick Warren states that "being successful and fulfilling your life's purpose are not at all the same issue! You could reach all your personal goals, becoming a raving success by the world's standard, and still miss the purposes for which God created you."[1]

Early in his earthly ministry Jesus spelled out God's expectations for every conceivable part of our lives in his most famous sermon, The Sermon on the Mount (Matthew 5:1—7:29). Jesus made it clear in that sermon that God's standards in no way, shape, or form match the world's standards. As a matter of fact, God's standards and expectations contradict and challenge the commonly accepted standards and values of the world. They turn the

1

world's standards upside down and inside out. The world says to take revenge on those who do us wrong; Jesus said to forgive them and be kind to them. The world says to hate our enemies; Jesus said to love them and pray for them. The world says to let people know the good things we've done so they will admire us; Jesus said to keep those good things secret. The world says to accumulate as much wealth and possessions as possible and hold onto them; Jesus said to give them away.

In addition, the world's currency has no value in God's economy. "'For the things that are considered of great value by man are worth nothing in God's sight'" (Luke 16:15 GNT). The world measures success according to wealth, power, fame, and status. God measures success according to the quality of our relationship with him (if we have one). "'A person is a fool to store up earthly wealth but not have a rich relationship with God'" (Luke 12:21). Further, God doesn't care how much money we have; he cares about what we do with our money. "'Guard against every kind of greed. Life is not measured by how much you own'" (Luke 12:15). The same holds true for power, fame, status, or influence. None of these things is inherently good or inherently bad. Any one of them can be used for good or used for bad.

The stories of multiple individuals are told in this book. Some achieved success according to the standards of the world, and some did not. Some lived a life of purpose, and some did not. Each story, however, touched me in a significant way. Taken together, they inspired, encouraged, challenged, affirmed, and comforted me. I hope they do the same for you.

Regardless of whether the individuals whose stories I chose to tell lived successful lives or lived purposeful lives, they share many of the same personality characteristics and behavior patterns. They also manifest some significant differences.

This book is about the similarities and differences between living a life of success and living a life of purpose. Success will be addressed first.

CHAPTER ONE

SUCCESS: A CHOICE

As one moves into adulthood, it is important to establish a firm foundation upon which to live one's adult life. Part of establishing that foundation is making decisions about one's adult lifestyle and values based on one's abilities, talents, interests, etc. In order to do this, one must separate from one's family of origin. The separation I am talking about here is an emotional separation, not a physical one. It has nothing to do with geography. It has to do with choices.

The choices and decisions we make are determined by the lens through which we view reality. Each of us, whether we are aware of it or not, views reality through a lens comprised of values and beliefs about ourselves and our world. The values and beliefs that comprise our lens have their roots in what we were taught and what we experienced in the family and culture we grew up in. Though we may not be aware of our lens, it is most definitely there, and it works powerfully. It filters what we see and determines what we think about what we see. This includes how we define success.

Note: Our purpose is not one of the elements that comprises our lens. Our purpose does not come from what we were taught and what we experienced in the family and culture we grew up in. Our purpose comes from God. He assigns it to us and designs us to be able to effectively fulfill it.

If a young adult makes choices regarding lifestyle and values to either please or spite parents, he or she has not adequately separated. In either of these scenarios, the parents' lifestyle and values are the starting point, not the individual's own abilities, talents, interests, etc. If a young adult does make these decisions with parental values as the starting point, however, all is not lost. One can do the emotional work necessary to separate at any point in his or her adult life and implement a course correction.

Regarding success, one can choose to adopt parents' and/or culture's definition of success because it fits one's own abilities, talents, interests, etc.; or one can choose to adopt parents' definition of success to please parents. On the other hand, one can choose a definition of success different from that of his or her parents to rebel against parents, or one can develop a definition of success that is different from one's parents' definition because it fits for him or her. The operative word here is *choose*.

The first step in this process is becoming aware of the lens through which you view the world. Once you are aware of your lens, you can choose to either keep the values and beliefs that comprise your lens, or you can choose to delete some or all of them and insert values and beliefs of your own choosing. Again, the operative word here is *choose*.

Choosing

Though many people in the world define and measure success according to the level of one's wealth, power, fame, and/ or status, these are not the criteria everyone uses to define and measure success. Some choose alternate definitions of success. Some of these alternate definitions are:

- "Success is having a place to call home." (Missy Yost)
- "Success is getting up one more time than you fall down." (Lina Ramos)
- "Success isn't about how much money you make. It's about the difference you make in people's lives." (Barack Obama)
- "Success is liking yourself, liking what you do, and liking how you do it." (Maya Angelou)
- "Success is the ability to go from one failure to another with no loss of enthusiasm." (Winston Churchill)
- "To laugh often and much; to win the respect of intelligent people and the affection of children; to earn the appreciation of honest critics and endure the betrayal of false friends; to appreciate beauty; to find the best in others; to leave the world a bit better, whether by a healthy child, a garden patch, or a redeemed social condition; to know even one life has breathed easier because you have lived. This is to have succeeded." (Ralph Waldo Emerson)

- "Success isn't how much money you have. Success is not what your position is. Success is how well you do what you do when nobody else is looking." (John Paul DeJoria)
- "Success is knowing your purpose in life, growing to reach your maximum potential, and sowing seeds that benefit others." (John C. Maxwell)

If you're unsure how to go about developing your own definition of success, Stephen Covey has a rather unique suggestion as to where you might start: "If you carefully consider what you want to be said of you in the funeral experience, you will find *your* definition of success."[2]

If one is to freely choose his or her definition of success, and then act on it, one has to embrace the belief that he or she *has* a choice; that he or she is in charge of their life and can set the direction or course of their life. If one does not embrace this belief, then he or she gives that choice away, allowing others to chart the course of their life.

Two individuals who embraced this belief and acted on it, charting the course of their own lives, were Howard Schultz and Bruce Springsteen. An individual who started on one road to success and, over time, implemented *two* course corrections was Theodore Roosevelt.

CHAPTER TWO

HOWARD'S STORY

Howard Schultz was born July 19, 1953, in New York City. He was raised in a low-income housing project in Brooklyn, the oldest of three children. His father, who had not finished high school, supported the family through a string of low paying blue-collar jobs, sometimes working two or three jobs just to meet expenses.

When Howard was seven years old, his father broke his hip and ankle at work. Decades later Howard wrote that

> in the 1960's, an uneducated, unskilled worker like my dad who got hurt on the job was typically dismissed without notice. The accident left my father with no income, no health insurance, no workers' compensation, and because my parents had no savings, they had nothing to fall back on. . . If not for a local charitable organization, Jewish Family Services, my family would have run out of food.[3]

He also wrote, "As a kid, I never had any idea that I would one day head a company. But I knew in my heart that if I was ever in a position where I could make a difference, I wouldn't leave people behind."[4]

In the years following his father's accident, the atmosphere in the home became quite contentious, primarily due to his parents' frequent arguments about money. To deal with the stress this caused, Howard turned to sports.

> I played sports with the neighborhood kids from dawn to dusk every day . . . Each Saturday and Sunday morning, starting at 8 A.M., hundreds of us kids would gather in the schoolyard. You had to be good there, because if you didn't win, you'd be out of the game, forced to watch for hours before you could get back in. So I played to win.[5]

This coping strategy, coupled with consistent and intentional encouragement from his mother, planted the seeds for his later success in life.

> In the 1950s and early 1960s, the American dream was vibrant, and we all felt entitled to a piece of it. My mother drummed that into us. She herself had never finished high school, and her biggest dream was a college education for all three of her kids . . . Over and over, she would put powerful models in front of me, pointing out individuals who had made something of their lives and insisting that I, too, could achieve

anything I set my heart on. She encouraged me to challenge myself, to place myself in situations that weren't comfortable, so that I could learn to overcome adversity . . . she willed us to succeed . . . I didn't know what work I would eventually do, but I knew I had to escape the struggle my parents lived with every day. I had to get out of the Projects, out of Brooklyn . . . I was aware of only one escape route: sports . . . In high school, I applied myself to school-work only when I had to, because what I learned in the classroom seemed irrelevant. Instead I spent hours and days playing football.[6]

Due to a natural athletic ability and his determination to find a way out of the Projects, this strategy worked for him. He was invited to Northern Michigan University to try out for their football team and promised a scholarship if he made the team. Unfortunately, he did not make the team. He didn't give up and go home, though. He stayed in school, supporting himself with student loans and multiple jobs throughout his college years. In writing about his time at Northern Michigan University, he stated "I began to figure out who I was away from my family."[7] This statement would seem to indicate that he separated emotionally, at least to some degree, from his parents. He graduated in 1975 and eventually returned to New York City, where he went to work for Xerox selling word processors.

He first learned of Starbucks in 1981 at a subsequent job with Hammarplast Corporation, selling kitchen equipment and housewares. "A little retailer in Seattle was placing unusually large orders for a certain type of drip coffeemaker . . . I investigated. Starbucks Coffee, Tea, and Spice had only four small stores then, yet it was buying this product in quantities larger than Macy's."[8] He was so curious that he went to Seattle to check out Starbucks. What he discovered there led him to implement a course correction that changed the trajectory of his life in a significant way.

A different kind of business

Howard learned that "the coffee I had been drinking was swill." He then "started asking questions about the company, about coffees from different regions of the world, about different ways of roasting coffee."[9] He met and spent time with the owners of the company, Jerry Baldwin and Gordon Bowker. "The founders of Starbucks were far from typical businessmen . . . None of them aspired to build a business empire. They founded Starbucks for one reason: They loved coffee and tea and wanted Seattle to have access to the best."[10] He went on to say, "I had never heard anyone talk about a product the way Jerry talked about coffee. He wasn't calculating how to maximize sales; he was providing people with something he believed they ought to enjoy. It was an approach to business, and to selling, that was as fresh and novel to me as the Starbucks coffee we were drinking."[11]

Over the next year Howard traveled to Seattle several times. He met with the owners of Starbucks each time, talking with them about what he could contribute to the company. He gradually convinced them to hire him. In September 1982 Howard and his wife left New York and moved to Seattle, where he assumed the position of marketing director at Starbucks. At that time Starbucks had five small retail stores in Seattle that sold whole bean coffee.

Passion awakened

In Spring 1983 Howard went to Italy. He spent time in Milan and Verona, where he discovered espresso bars. They seemed to be on every corner. He described his experience in Italy in the following words:

> To the Italians, the coffee bar is not a diner, as coffee shops came to be in America in the 1950s and 1960s. It is an extension of the front porch, an extension of the home. Each morning they stop at their favorite coffee bar, where they're treated with a cup of espresso that they know is custom-made . . . As I watched, I had a revelation: Starbucks had missed the point—completely missed it. *This is so powerful!* I thought. *This is the link.* The connection to the people who loved coffee did not have to take place only in their homes, where they ground and brewed whole-bean coffee. What we had to do was unlock the romance and mystery of coffee, firsthand, in coffee bars. The Italians understood the personal relationship that people could have to coffee, it's social aspect. I couldn't believe that Starbucks was in the coffee business, yet was overlooking so central an element of it. It was like an epiphany. It was so immediate and physical that I was shaking

... The Italians had turned the drinking of coffee into a symphony, and it felt right. Starbucks was playing in the same hall, but we were playing without a string section.[12]

Howard brought his vision, along with the excitement and passion the vision evoked, of what Starbucks could be back to Seattle. When he shared his vision with his bosses, however, they did not embrace it. They saw Starbucks as a retailer and wanted it to remain a retailer. Over the next two years Howard and Jerry Baldwin engaged in countless discussions about the future of Starbucks. In late 1985 it finally became crystal clear that they were not going to share the same vision for the company, so they amicably parted ways. Howard left Starbucks and started his own company, Il Giornale. "From its inception, Il Giornale was intended to be a major enterprise, not just a single store."[13]

In March 1987 Jerry Baldwin and Gordon Bowker decided to sell the Starbucks stores in Seattle, the roasting plant, and the Starbucks name, and Howard decided to buy it. At that time Starbucks had six stores and Il Giornale had three. After raising the capital he needed, Howard purchased Starbucks in August 1987 and gave Il Giornale the Starbucks name. He was chairman and chief executive officer of the Starbucks Corporation until 2000.

Under his leadership Starbucks grew exponentially. In speaking of the remarkable growth of Starbucks, Howard stated, "Many of the values that shaped the growth of the enterprise trace their roots back to a crowded apartment in Brooklyn, New York."[14]

From the beginning, I wanted to create a business model that was different from the command-and-control relationship between employers and employees during my dad's working years. I never shook off the indelible image of my father immobile on the couch after he slipped on the ice, helpless and abandoned by the company he was working for when the accident occurred. Workers deserved a different relationship to the companies they helped to build, one based on trust, mutual care, and honesty.[15]

These values and guiding principles led Howard to convince the board of directors to offer full medical benefits to part-timers in late 1988. The benefits included preventive care, crisis counseling, mental health, chemical dependency, and vision and dental coverage. The company paid 75% of the coverage, leaving only 25% to be paid by the employee. In 1991 the benefit package was expanded to cover any employee diagnosed with a terminal illness. The company covered 100% of the employee's medical costs from the time he or she was no longer able to work until the person was eligible for government benefits.

My view of a successful business wasn't just measured in number of stores. I wanted to create a brand name respected for the best in coffee and a well-run company admired for its corporate responsibility. I wanted to elevate the enterprise to a higher standard, to make our people proud of working for a company that cared for them and gave back to their community . . . I wanted to build a company that would thrive for years because its competitive advantage was based on its values and guiding principles.[16]

He also convinced the Board of Directors to offer Bean Stock, the company's stock option plan, to all employees who had been there six months, including part-timers who worked 20 hours per week. In 1991, when Bean Stock was first offered, the employees stopped being employees and became partners.

Bean Stock was a chance to elevate people's lives. As the company's value grew, so did the value of our shares and partners' sense of security, as well as the choices and options they had for themselves and their families . . . The stock's increasing market value has helped people build retirement savings as well as put down payments on houses, afford college, pay off debt, take vacations, or start their own businesses.[17]

No one was left behind.

An ending and a beginning

In June 2000 Howard stepped down as CEO and moved into the new position of chief global strategist to help Starbucks expand internationally. In January 2008, he stepped back into the position of CEO due to his concern regarding the company's downhill slide. He believed a major contributing factor to this downhill slide was that the company had distanced itself from the values and guiding principles upon which it had been founded.

When he returned as CEO, he brought the company back to the basics, once again leading it according to its original values and guiding principles. One of the first things he did was close 7,100 stores in the United States on the same day in February 2008 to retrain 135,000 baristas in the art of making espresso.

He also convinced the board of directors to approve a leadership conference (the previous year's annual leadership conference had been canceled to help pay for raises for store employees). Getting the approval for a leadership conference that would cost the company approximately $30 million at a time when they needed to reduce expenses was not an easy sell; however, Howard believed it was critical. He was convinced the store managers needed to understand that the survival of the company was at stake and that they were part of the solution; i.e., every store needed to increase sales and profits to get the company back on track, and managers needed to take responsibility for their store's performance.

The conference was approved, and in October 2008 ten thousand store managers descended on New Orleans for the four-day conference. Over the course of that four days the managers were immersed in multiple experiences that would facilitate their reconnection to the company's core purpose, i.e., "to achieve that fragile balance between profitability and social responsibility."[18] They were reminded that "each customer deserved the perfect beverage and to be treated as a human being in a world that could feel dehumanizing."[19] In order to achieve this, the managers were instructed to give baristas permission to do whatever was right for a customer—for example, to pour out a beverage if it was not made to a customer's specification and make a new one. "After the conference, thousands of managers returned to their stores across the country with more than new expertise. Many believed that they had the potential to help turn the company around. They also had the desire to do so."[20]

Turning the company around

In order to make the company profitable again, many difficult and pain-causing decisions needed to be made. These decisions included firing executives and closing stores that were not performing according to needed standards. One decision that was made that alleviated, rather than causing, pain was to maintain the current level of health insurance benefits. Howard insisted on this in spite of being urged to reduce the benefits. He stated that

> eliminating or reducing healthcare for our partners could immediately boost profits . . . But it would be utterly unfair to thousands of people and their families, and verge on inhumane. It would also sap spirits and breach trust. I knew we'd never recover . . . eliminating healthcare coverage was not an option . . . Despite the immediate financial gains, not every decision we made could be economic."[21]

As Starbucks began to be profitable again, the company's focus on social responsibility became more prominent. In the ensuing years Starbucks, under Howard's leadership,

- Launched CreateJobsforUSA. In fall 2011, due to approximately 14 million people being unemployed at that time, Starbucks raised money by selling wristbands with the word *INDIVISIBLE* imprinted on them in their stores in the United States. The money was then donated to Community Development Financial Institution, which "lent money to start-ups, small businesses, housing projects and nonprofit organizations in low-income areas throughout the country."[22] This initiative raised $15.2 million, which "helped create or sustain more than five thousand jobs."[23]

- In 2013, due to a large number of military personnel returning from Afghanistan who were having difficulty finding employment, committed to building stores on or near military bases that would be staffed solely by veterans or spouses of active duty military personnel. By 2017 Starbucks had hired ten thousand veterans and military spouses, and by 2018 there were 45 stores in 21 states staffed by military personnel.

- Partnered with Arizona State University in 2014 to create the Starbucks College Achievement Plan, allowing Starbucks partners to attend ASU's online university. Initially, the plan covered 100% of tuition cost for all Starbucks partners who were college juniors and seniors. Partial tuition coverage was available for partners who were freshman and sophomores. In addition, each student was paired with three advisors: a financial coach, an academic advisor, and a success coach. The role of the success coach was to "check in periodically, email reminders about university deadlines, offer encouragement after a tough test, celebrate good grades, and suggest ways to reduce stress and balance school and life".[24] The plan was later expanded so freshmen and sophomores could also receive full tuition coverage, and partners who were veterans could receive tuition coverage for a spouse or a child. By 2017 Starbucks had made it possible for one thousand individuals to graduate from college.
- Increased the number of stores in low- and middle-income areas. "One role of the stores was to employ young people from the community and offer spaces for them to receive job training."[25]

- Launched the 10,000 Opportunities Initiative in Spring 2015 because an estimated 5.6 million Americans between the ages of 16 and 24 were reportedly neither in school nor employed. Starbucks built a coalition of corporations and private foundations to decrease this number. The Initiative kicked off in August 2015 with a job fair at the McCormick Place Convention Center in Chicago. For two weeks prior to the job fair, several pre-fair workshops were offered to young people to help them prepare a resume and practice interviewing. More than 30 companies participated in the job fair, which was attended by approximately 4000 young people. On the day of the job fair more than 600 individuals received job offers. Over the next two years job fairs were held in six more cities.

Howard stepped down as CEO of Starbucks in April 2017. He moved into the position of executive chairman, overseeing Starbucks's social impact work and opening new stores around the world. In 2018, he exited Starbucks completely.

CHAPTER THREE

BRUCE'S STORY

Bruce Springsteen was born September 23, 1949, in Long Branch, New Jersey, and raised in the neighboring town of Freehold. His father had a blue-collar job at Ford. His mother worked as a legal secretary. In his autobiography, *Born to Run*, Bruce wrote,

> We were pretty near poor, though I never thought about it. We were clothed, fed and bedded. I had white and black friends worse off . . . Our house was old and soon to be noticeably decrepit. One kerosene stove in the living room was all we had to heat the whole place. Upstairs, where my family slept, you woke on winter mornings with your breath visible."[26]

Bruce, his parents, and his two younger sisters lived with his paternal grandparents. The atmosphere in the home was troubled due to blurred generational boundaries, mental illness, and his father's excessive use of alcohol. His grandmother, beginning at Bruce's birth, assumed the role of mother with an uncompromising and immovable stance.

In an effort to keep the peace, neither of Bruce's parents challenged her.

During his preschool years Bruce experienced limitless freedom. The schedules, routines, and rules that most preschool children grow up with were totally absent. Therefore, when he entered the local Catholic elementary school, functioning within the required structure was extremely difficult for him, and he rebelled against it.

> Before my grammar school education was over I'd have my knuckles classically rapped, my tie pulled 'til I choked; be struck in the head, shut into a dark closet and stuffed into a trash can while being told this is where I belonged. All business as usual in Catholic school in the fifties.[27]

The lighting of a fire

On a Sunday night in 1956 at age seven Bruce watched Elvis Presley on the *Ed Sullivan Show*, and a fire started in the core of his being that never burned out.

> When it was over that night, those few minutes, when the man with the guitar vanished in a shroud of screams, I sat there transfixed in front of the television set, my mind on fire. I had the same two arms, two legs, two eyes; I looked hideous but I'd figure that part out ... so what was missing? THE GUITAR!! He was hitting it, leaning on it, dancing with it, screaming into it, screwing it, caressing it, swinging it on his hips and, once in a while, even

playing it! The master key, the sword in the stone, the sacred talisman, the staff of righteousness, the greatest instrument of seduction the teenage world had ever known, the . . ."ANSWER" to my alienation and sorrow, it was a reason to live, to try to communicate with the other poor souls stuck in the same position I was.[28]

The next day his mother rented a guitar for him. He took a few weeks of lessons and quit. Before he returned the guitar, he held a concert for some neighborhood children in his backyard. Later that same day he returned the guitar and said, "It was over for now, but for a moment, just a moment, in front of those kids in my backyard . . . I smelled blood."[29]

Over the next however many years he immersed himself in the music of the late fifties and early sixties via the radio in his home and in his parents' car, and on the jukebox at a local luncheonette. Then "The Beatles. I first laid ears on them while driving with my mom up South Street, the radio burning brighter before my eyes as it strained to contain the sound, the harmonies of 'I Want to Hold Your Hand.' Why did it sound so different? Why was it so good? Why was I this excited?"[30] The excitement lasted for months as

Every Wednesday night I sat up in my room charting the weekly top twenty and if the Beatles were not firmly ensconced each week as lords of all radio, it would drive me nuts . . . I lived for every Beatles record release. I searched the newsstands for every magazine with a photo

I hadn't seen and I dreamed . . . dreamed . . . dreamed . . . that it was me . . . It didn't take me long to figure it out: I didn't want to meet the Beatles. I wanted to BE the Beatles.[31]

In order to BE the Beatles, he would have to have a guitar and would have to know how to play it. He earned money to purchase a guitar by mowing lawns and painting a neighbor's house. A cousin showed him how to tune the guitar and read chords. He eventually learned most of the chords and how to put them together to be able to play a song. He then decided that he needed an electric guitar. He came up with half the needed funds by selling a pool table he owned. His mother came up with the other half. Soon he was the owner of a Kent electric guitar and was jamming at a friend's house with other young musicians. They eventually evolved into a band.

One day our young combo heard of Sunday matinee shows for teenagers at the Freehold Elks Club . . . it was a good place for your first baptism by fire . . . With anxiety somewhere around pre-Super Bowl levels, my bandmates and I loaded our gear into our parents' cars, hauled it down to the Elks and set up . . . We spun through our tunes; panic and cold sweat aside, we weren't bad.[32]

They were then booked to play for a school dance. When that gig was over, he was voted out of the band by his bandmates.

Watching and learning

That night I went home, pulled out the second
Rolling Stones album, put it on and taught
myself Keith Richards's simple but great guitar
solo to "It's All Over Now." It took me all night
but by midnight I had a reasonable facsimile of
it down . . . I was going to play lead guitar. For
the next several months (years!) I woodshedded,
spending every available hour cradling my Kent,
twisting and torturing the strings 'til they broke
or until I fell back on my bed asleep with it in
my arms. Weekends I spent at the local CYO,
YMCA or high school dances . . . I was silent,
inscrutable, arms folded, standing in front of
the lead guitarist of whatever band was playing,
watching every move his fingers made. After the
dance . . . I rushed home to my room and there
'til early in the morning, my guitar unplugged so
as not to disturb the house, I tried to remember
and play everything I'd seen. Before long I began
to feel the empowerment the instrument and my
work were bringing me. I had a secret . . . there
was *something* I could do, something I might be
good at. I fell asleep at night with dreams of rock
'n' roll glory in my head.[33]

After a while he was invited to join a band that was
forming in his hometown, the Castiles. Their first gig
was a summer party at a local trailer park where they

played to approximately 50 people. "It was a huge success, convinced us we could make music and put on a show . . . I still remember the exhilaration . . . we moved people; we brought the energy and an hour or so of good times. We made raw, rudimentary, local but effective magic."[34]

> From there on out it was YMCAs, CYOs, high schools, ice rinks, roller rinks, VFW halls, battles of the bands, Elks clubs, supermarket openings, officers' clubs, drive-in theaters, mental hospitals, beach clubs and any place you could set up a five-piece band that wanted decent local entertainment at a cheap price.[35]

In the late sixties he met Steve Van Zandt, who was then with a band called Shadows.

> Over the next years we would visit each other's gigs often . . . We formed a mutual admiration society of two. I'd finally met someone who felt about music the way I did, needed it the way I did, respected its power in a way that was a notch above the attitudes of the other musicians I'd come in contact with, somebody I understood and I felt understood me.[36]

In 1968 the Castiles made a decision that, in order to be discovered, they needed to expand their horizon beyond New Jersey. They managed to get a booking at a café in Greenwich Village in New York City. Following that performance, he and Steve traveled to that café many times to watch and listen to bands, learning from them. "The bus trips became a regular part of our weekends . . . It became our true home away from home . . . the Castiles played regularly on Saturday and Sunday next door to the Fugs on MacDougal Street."[37]

An ending and a beginning
The summer after he graduated from high school,

> The Freehold Police Department swept up more than half the Castiles in the town's first drug crackdown . . . It was a town scandal, trouble all around and the finale of the Castiles' great three-year run . . . The group I'd taken my first baby steps with and strutted my way to small-town guitar-slinging glory was over. There would be no encore.[38]

He then formed another band, who became "the monster rock kings of our piece of the shore"[39] (Asbury Park, New Jersey). At one of these gigs Bruce was approached by a record producer. He invited Bruce to his studio to watch a recording session. "I sat in the darkness of a real studio and watched an actual recording session being conducted. I left that night finally feeling a musical future in front of me."[40]

During the time (late1960s) that Bruce was trying to break into the music industry, the Vietnam war was in full swing. One fateful day he found a draft notice in his mailbox. When he reported for his physical, he was judged unfit for military service. He dodged that bullet, maybe literally, and continued on with his music.

The first time he played in Asbury Park, he jammed with two musicians he didn't know.

> I watched people sit up, move closer and begin to pay serious attention. I saw two guys pull chairs onto the middle of the dance floor and sit themselves down in them, arms folded across their chest, as if to say, "Bring it on," and I brought it . . . I made some new friends that night . . . had my first conversation with a freckle-faced Danny Federici . . . ran into Vincent Lopez . . . we all gathered with bass player Little Vinnie Roslin . . . and started working. This was the band that would initially call itself Child, then morph into Steel Mill, then the Bruce Springsteen Band, and eventually become the core of the original E Street Band.[41]

When Bruce was 19, his parents decided to move to California. Though they asked him to go with them, he chose to stay in New Jersey to pursue his music and fend for himself. Fending for himself meant at times sharing a room with a buddy, at times sleeping on someone's couch or floor, and at times sleeping on the beach, all while pursuing his dreams of rock 'n' roll glory.

"We played the bars and night clubs of the late-sixties shore. We played original music with some covers, and the simple fact that we were so good was all that kept us working . . . Our ability to excite and entertain, and having our craft down cold, kept us alive."[42]

Starting to grow

They began to attract bigger crowds, too big for bars. They began to play in parks and at colleges, first at the Jersey shore and then in Richmond, Virginia. They gradually expanded into Nashville, Tennessee, and Chapel Hill, North Carolina. In 1970, when Bruce was 21, he and his bandmates drove cross country to play a New Year's Eve party in Big Sur, California. They then spent a few weeks in San Francisco, where they managed to get a few bookings opening for some headliners and playing at a club. The opportunities then dried up, and as there were no more on the horizon, they drove cross country again back to New Jersey.

On the long drive home, Bruce reflected on what he had seen, heard, and learned in California.

> I came up against some real talent and held my own, but . . . They had something we didn't, a certain level of sophisticated musicality. They were better than us and that didn't sit well with me. It's not that I didn't expect to come up against superior talent; that happens, it's the way God planned it. I was fast, but like the old gunslingers knew, there's always somebody faster, and if you can do it better than me, you earn my respect and admiration and you inspire me to work harder. I wasn't afraid of that. I was concerned with not maximizing my own abilities, not having a broad or intelligent enough vision of what I was capable of. I was all I had. I had only one talent. I was not a natural genius. I would have to use

every ounce of what was in me—my cunning, my musical skills, my showmanship, my intellect, my heart, my willingness—night after night, to push myself harder, to work with more intensity than the next guy just to survive untended in the world I lived in.[43]

When they got back to New Jersey the band, Steel Mill by this time, decided to vote out bass player Vinnie Roslin and replace him with Steve Van Zandt. The band then played regularly in New Jersey and in Richmond.

Changes

Bruce eventually changed his style of music. This led to changing the four-person rock band into a "ten-piece horns-and-singers-augmented rock and soul band playing nothing but new original music."[44] It also led to the name of the band changing from Steel Mill to the Bruce Springsteen Band. This in turn meant a change in the power structure within the band.

I'd declared democracy and band names dead after Steel Mill. I was leading the band, playing, singing and writing everything we did. If I was going to carry the workload and responsibility, I might as well assume the power . . . I look back on this as being one of the smartest decisions of my young life. I've always believed the E Street Band's continued existence . . . is partially due to the fact that there was little to no role confusion amongst its members. Everyone knew their job, their boundaries, their blessings and limitations. My bandmates were not always happy with the decisions I made and may have been angered by some of them, but nobody debated my right to make them. Clarity ruled and allowed us to forge a bond based on the principle that we worked together, but it was my band. I crafted a benevolent dictatorship; creative input was welcomed within the structure I prepared but it was my name on the dotted line and on the records.[45]

The road they traveled was far from smooth after these changes were made. Their fans did not embrace their new style of music. They lost bookings and struggled financially. This necessitated letting go of some of the new band members. Bruce and Steve then found a bar in Asbury Park that was not doing well at the height of the summer season. They convinced the owner to let them play. The arrangement was that the owner would pay them nothing, would charge a $1.00 cover charge at the door, and the band would get 100% of the cover charge. The first night they played to 15 people. The second night to 30 people, and the third night to 80 people. They quickly worked their way up to playing three nights a week to 150 people each night.

When the summer ended, so did the gig. Bruce decided to go back to California, but this time he went alone. He spent three weeks trying to earn money playing music but was unsuccessful. So, back to New Jersey he went. When he got there, he again had difficulty earning money. He then decided to take a break from playing music and spent his time and energy writing songs.

BIG changes

After he'd written a few songs he contacted a record producer he had met in New York City, Mike Appel, and played the new songs for him. Mike liked the new songs and Bruce contracted with Mike to be his manager. Mike arranged for Bruce to audition for John Hammond of Columbia Records. This resulted in a recording contract. The result was *Greetings from Asbury Park*, Bruce's first record. *Greetings* was released on January 5, 1973, and the band went out on tour.

> On stages across America we were cheered, were occasionally booed, dodged Frisbees from the audience, received rave reviews and were trashed … As far as I was concerned, it was the life. There would be no nine-to-five world for me, just a long, often arduous but who's-kidding-who free ride of a seven-day weekend . . . I was twenty-three and I was making a living playing music![46]

Greetings "sold about twenty-three thousand copies; that was a flop by record company standards but a smash by mine."[47] Also in 1973, while still touring, they recorded *The Wild, the Innocent and the E Street Shuffle*. The sales for this album were substantially lower than those for *Greetings*.

> At the time of *The Wild, the Innocent*, I had no success, so I had no real concerns about where

I was going. I was going up, I hoped, or at least out. With a record contract and a touring band, I felt I was better off than most of my friends, who were locked down in the nine-to-five world of responsibility and bills. I was lucky to be doing what I loved most.[48]

During this tour he met Jon Landau in Boston. Jon would eventually become his manager, replacing Mike Appel.

The next album, *Born to Run*, was released on August 25, 1975, and was "the record that would put us on the map"[49] and put Bruce on the cover of *Time* and *Newsweek* magazines. Simultaneous with the release of *Born to Run*, they played at the Bottom Line in New York City. "For five nights, two shows a night, we left everything we had on the tiny stage at 15 West Fourth Street . . . inside the band and on the street, you could feel the whole thing taking off."[50]

Born to Run eventually sold six million copies in the United States, and the tour that followed the release of the record marked them not as an up-and-coming rock band but as "a new young force to be reckoned with."[51]

Darkness on the Edge of Town was the next album, released on June 2, 1978, followed by another tour. *The River*, released October 17, 1980, was "the album where the E Street Band hit its stride, striking the perfect balance between a garage band and the professionalism required to make good records."[52] *Nebraska* was next, released September 30, 1982. No tour followed.

Taking care of business

Following the recording and mixing of *Nebraska*, Bruce took some time off to take care of personal business. His experiences in his childhood home and elementary school had left him with many internal emotional wounds and conflicts. He was able to keep these out of his conscious awareness and under wraps for a long time with his music. He stated,

> It had long ago become the way I channeled just about any and all information I received from living on planet Earth . . . that's how I used my music and my talents from the very beginning. As a salve, a balm, a tool to tease out the clues to the unknowable in my life. It was the fundamental why and wherefore of my picking up the guitar.[53]

Songwriting gave him an outlet to express his thoughts and feelings about his experiences. Performing was his medication to ease the pain.

Throughout his career Bruce has been known for performing concerts that lasted longer than those played by most, if not all, of his contemporaries in the music industry. In *Born to Run* he wrote about what performing is like for him:

> I never really had the ease or ability to enjoy myself very freely . . . I was always proud but also embarrassed by being so in control . . . never regularly quite had the mojo to freely let the "bon temps rouler." Except . . . onstage. There, strangely enough, exposed in front of thousands,

I've always felt perfectly safe, to just let it all go. That's why at our shows you can't get rid of me.[54]

He also wrote that

there's a reason they don't call it "working," it's called PLAYING! . . . It's a life-giving, joyful, sweat-drenched, muscle-aching, voice-blowing, mind-clearing, exhausting, soul-invigorating, cathartic pleasure and privilege every night. You can sing about your misery, the world's misery, your most devastating experiences, but there is something in the gathering of souls that blows the blues away. Something that lets some sun in, that keeps you breathing, that lifts you in a way that can't be explained, only experienced. It's something to live for, and it was my lifeline to the rest of humanity in the days when those connections were tough for me to make.[55]

Interesting Note: Bruce, unlike many other rockers, did not engage in drug use.

Sobriety became a religion of sorts to me and I mistrusted those who treated the lack thereof as something to rally around and celebrate . . . I never cared for any kind of out-of-control "stonedness" around me. It brought back too many memories of unpredictable and quietly volatile evenings at home. Evenings of never knowing where I stood. I could never be completely at ease, or relaxed, as a young man in my own home . . . I don't know why, but I've never gotten anywhere near as far or as high as when I count the band in and feel what seems like all life itself and a small flash of eternity pulsing through me.[56]

In the days and weeks following the completion of *Nebraska*, there were no songs to write and no concerts to perform. The wounds and conflicts that had been kept under wraps so carefully for so long erupted to the surface. He wrote,

> My well of emotion is no longer being channeled and safely pipelined to the surface . . . my depression is spewing like an oil spill all over the beautiful turquoise-green gulf of my carefully planned and controlled existence. It's black sludge is threatening to smother every last living part of me.[57]

For the first time in his life he sought professional help. After a few weeks his symptoms improved to the point that allowed him to function again. He then began "one of the biggest adventures of my life, canvassing the squirrely terrain inside my own head for signs of life. *Life*–not a song, not a performance, not a story, but a *life*."[58]

He went on to say,

> I slowly acquired the skills that would eventually lead to a life of my own . . . over many meetings and long-distance phone calls during the next

twenty-five years Doc Myers and I would fight many demons together until his passing in 2008. When I was in town, we would sit face-to-face, with me staring into his understanding eyes patiently, painstakingly putting together a pretty good string of wins, along with some nagging defeats. We successfully slowed down that treadmill I'd been running on while never getting it to completely stop.[59]

The next album, *Born in the USA*, was released on June 4, 1984, and the band, once again, went out on tour. On June 1,1985, Bruce Springsteen and the E Street Band played their first stadium show in Dublin, Ireland, to 95 thousand people. The tour ended on September 27, to a crowd of 80 thousand in Los Angeles. By the time the tour ended they had most definitely become one of the most dominant and influential rock bands in the world.

Bruce was 34 years old when *Born in the USA*, which eventually sold 30 million copies worldwide, was released. This record, and the tour that followed it, elevated Bruce Springsteen to the height of superstardom, where he has remained, writing, recording, performing, and earning many awards along the way. The awards include 20 Grammys and an Academy Award. He is also the recipient of the Kennedy Center Honors and the Presidential Medal of Freedom. He has been inducted into the Rock and Roll Hall of Fame, the Songwriters Hall of Fame, and the New Jersey Hall of Fame.

CHAPTER FOUR

THEODORE'S STORY

As stated previously, anyone can effect one or more course corrections in his or her life. Theodore Roosevelt, the 26th President of the United States, is an example of someone who implemented two course corrections in his professional life. His first course correction involved his choice of profession. His second determined how he was going to use the influence inherent in various positions he held.

Roosevelt served as president from 1901–1909. Prior to his presidency he served as a New York State Assemblyman, federal Civil Service Commissioner, New York City Police Commissioner, Assistant Secretary of the Navy, Governor of New York, and United States Vice President.

Beginnings

Theodore Roosevelt was born October 27, 1858, and raised in a wealthy, privileged family in New York City. Both of his parents, Theodore Roosevelt Sr. and Martha Bulloch Roosevelt, had also grown up in wealthy, privileged families—Theodore Sr. in New York City and Martha in Roswell, Georgia.

When he reached college age Theodore entered Harvard. It's interesting to note that he held back from initiating friendships with fellow students until he could determine whether their families were of the same social and economic standing as his own. Once he verified this, he reached out to those students and eventually established several genuine friendships. He graduated in 1880 magna cum laude and Phi Beta Kappa, 21st in a class of 177. Following his graduation from Harvard, he entered Columbia Law School. He gradually became convinced, however, that a career in law was not a good fit for him. In his second year he dropped out of law school to run for public office (first course correction).

> The road that would lead Roosevelt into public life began at Morton Hall, the "barn-like room over a saloon" at 59th Street and Fifth Avenue that served as the Republican headquarters for the Twenty-first District . . . When he began inquiring about the local Republican organization, he was warned by his privileged circle that district politics were "low," the province of "saloon-keepers, horse-car conductors, and the like," men who "would be rough and brutal and unpleasant to deal with." Their caution did nothing to deter Roosevelt . . . In addition to attending the monthly meetings, Roosevelt stopped by in the evenings at the smoke-filled room with its benches, cuspidors,

and poker tables . . . To the machine politicians who represented the tenement population, Roosevelt initially appeared very much an alien . . . Over time, however . . . he won over his comrades with the warmth, unabashed intensity, and pluck of his personality. He particularly grew close to Joe Murray . . . When an assembly seat came open in 1881 Murray nominated Roosevelt. The shrewd boss calculated that victory over the Democratic candidate would be assured if the Republican machine mustered its regular totals while Roosevelt mobilized the college-educated men and the "swells" who rarely voted in local elections. Murray's instincts proved correct . . . Theodore Roosevelt was elected as the youngest member of the New York State Assembly.[60]

He immediately made his presence known in the Assembly when he assumed a lead role in the battle to impeach a corrupt state Supreme Court judge, Theodore Westbrook.

In December 1881 the *New York Times* had run an article alleging that Judge Westbrook aided Wall Street financier Jay Gould in an illegal takeover of Manhattan Elevated Railway Company. The *Times* reported that Gould's partners devised a lawsuit that forced the Manhattan Elevated Railway Company into receivership.

Note: According to Wikipedia, receivership is "the situation in which an institution or enterprise is being held by a receiver, a person placed in the custodial responsibility for the property of others, including tangible and intangible assets and rights, especially in cases where a company cannot meet its financial obligations or enters bankruptcy."

Judge Westbrook became the receiver for the company.

> Holding court in Gould's private offices, Westbrook issued a series of onerous rulings calculated to panic stockholders into throwing their shares on the market, depressing the stock to almost nothing. At that point, the Gould syndicate began buying. Once Gould had gained control of the valuable property, Judge Westbrook mysteriously decreed the company solvent, and the stock rose sharply. This simple, perfidious maneuver cost thousands of innocent stockholders their life savings.[61]

Stepping into the fray

Roosevelt took on the battle after the *New York Herald* ran an article in March 1882 "accusing Judge Westbrook of a flagrant abuse of power and conflict of interest. He had appointed receivers for defunct insurance companies and granted excessive fees to select lawyers (including his cousin and son), who handled the cases."[62]

On March 29, 1882, Roosevelt introduced a resolution to the assembly to authorize the Judiciary Committee to investigate Westbrook. The resolution was stalled by assemblymen loyal to Westbrook and Gould. Roosevelt re-introduced the resolution one week later. Once again it was stalled. The same thing happened the third time he brought the resolution before the assembly. They then adjourned for Easter recess, during which time the newspapers continued to run the story. When the assembly reconvened, the resolution came to a vote and was passed by a sizable majority. One assembly man commented that, "by the time the Legislature came back again, the Legislators had evidently heard from their home folks, because the vote was overwhelmingly in favor of the investigation."[63]

Once the resolution to investigate Westbrook was passed, a seven-week investigation by the Judiciary Committee ensued, the result of which was that, "despite an accumulation of damaging evidence, a majority declared that Judge Westbrook's behavior, although indiscreet, did not warrant impeachment."[64] On May 31, 1882, the assembly voted to accept the Committee's report and exonerated Judge Westbrook.

The reaction of the press was as follows:

- *New York Times*: "It was apparent to those familiar with politics, that every wire that could be pulled in both the dominant political parties to prevent impeachment was stretched to the tautest."
- *New York Herald*: "The action of the Assembly last night in voting to exonerate Judge Westbrook is simply disgraceful."
- *Brooklyn Eagle* called the vote "an open avowal of contempt for public sentiment, for public intelligence and common honesty."

Roosevelt was re-elected to the assembly in November 1882. He served there until 1884. During that legislative session Roosevelt's view on labor laws began to shift. Due to his privileged upbringing and Ivy League education, he was a firm believer in the laissez-faire doctrine. According to the Merriam-Webster Dictionary, the laissez-faire doctrine is "a doctrine opposing governmental interference in economic affairs beyond the minimum necessary for the maintenance of peace and property rights."

During the early part of the legislative session, Roosevelt "voted against increasing the minimum wage to 25 cents an hour, spoke in opposition to a bill that would limit streetcar conductors to twelve-hour workdays, and fought against legislation to raise the salaries of New York's policemen and firemen."[65]

Starting to shift

His views began to shift when he explored the reasons behind the Cigar-Makers Union proposing legislation to stop the manufacture of cigars in tenement houses. He read a report written by labor leader Samuel Gompers that vividly described the conditions in these tenement houses and then went on a tour of the tenements with Gompers. The words Roosevelt read and the sights he saw forever changed his opinion regarding legislation aimed at protecting workers. He read,

> In one tenement house, fifteen families crowded into three floors. Fathers, mothers, and children were at work stripping, drying, and wrapping cigars from six in the morning until midnight. In

the yard, a breeding ground of disease with no drain
to a sewer, lay large mounds of decaying tobacco.
Another building housed ninety-eight people
from twenty families, with several families living
and working together in one room. Everywhere
piles of tobacco and fetid tobacco scraps littered
the floors, filling the air with an overwhelming
stench. The hallways were so dark and gloomy that
even at midday it seemed like night.[66]

He saw that

While a few of the tenements provided living
space for the workers apart from the sweatshops,
the overwhelming majority had no separate
accommodation. He long remembered one
tenement in which five adults and several children
were confined to a single room for sleeping, eating,
and making cigars. The tobacco was stowed about
everywhere, alongside the foul bedding and in a
corner where there were scraps of food.[67]

Though the proposed bill certainly went against the
laissez-faire doctrine in which he thoroughly believed,
Roosevelt wholeheartedly supported it. The bill did pass
and became law in March 1883.

His new views and beliefs regarding the need for
legislation aimed at protecting workers were cemented
when the cigar makers brought suit against the new law,
"arguing their right to hold property, guaranteed by the
state constitution, was violated by the new regulations."[68]

The New York Court of Appeals found in favor of the cigar makers.

> "It was this case," Roosevelt later said, "which first waked me to . . . the fact that the courts were not necessarily the best judges of what should be done to better social and industrial conditions." While the justices were well intentioned, they interpreted law solely from the vantage point of the propertied classes. "They knew nothing whatever of tenement house conditions," he charged, "they knew nothing whatever of the needs, or of the life and labor, of three-fourths of their fellow citizens in great cities."[69]

ꝰ Second course correction

From this point on, Roosevelt focused his boundless energy while in public office working tirelessly to improve conditions for the working class, no longer using the laissez-faire doctrine as his guiding principle for legislation. In doing so, he was continuously fighting against corrupt politicians and robber barons. He seems to have been driven by a deep compassion for the horrendous life circumstances of many laborers, coupled with outrage at the robber barons, who profited greatly from their labor and who sabotaged efforts to improve their circumstances.

Robber barons were, according to Wikipedia, "businessmen who used what were considered to be exploitative practices to amass their wealth. These practices included exerting control over national resources, accruing high levels of government influence, paying extremely low wages, squashing competition by acquiring competitors in order to create monopolies and eventually raise prices, and schemes to sell stock at inflated prices to unsuspecting investors in a manner which would eventually destroy the company for which the stock was issued and impoverish investors."

It is important to remember that when he made this course correction he was no longer in step with individuals in his circle of friends, acquaintances, and associates.

From 1889 until 1895 he served in the federal government as Civil Service Commissioner. The primary responsibility of the civil service commissioner was "enforcing the 1883 Pendleton Act, mandating that one quarter of all federal jobs be filled by competitive examination rather than party affiliation."[70] While serving in this role, Roosevelt attempted to enforce the Pendleton Act by demanding that government jobs be given to individuals based on merit rather than as a reward for supporting a political campaign. Though his efforts achieved some successes regarding specific appointments, he was unable to significantly impact the underlying system of corruption.

Roosevelt went from the position of Civil Service Commissioner to that of President of the Board of New York City Police Commissioners. When Roosevelt stepped into that role, he was walking into a "vast entrenched system of police corruption that would not yield so easily to reform."[71] The system "allowed those businesses willing to pay Tammany Hall's substantial monthly charge to operate unmolested, while those who refused to furnish protection money were closed down."[72]

Note: Wikipedia describes Tammany Hall as "the Democratic Party political machine that played a major role in controlling New York City and New York State politics and helping immigrants, most notably the Irish, rise up in American politics . . . served as an engine for graft and political corruption."

"New police recruits were forced to pay Tammany a fixed fee for their appointments . . . every officer understood he would make the money back with plenty to spare once inside the system . . . each advancement required hefty additional fees . . . With each higher rank a policeman attained, his percentage of the blackmail fund grew."[73]

At his first press conference, Roosevelt stated that, beginning immediately, appointments and promotions would be made solely on merit. The police force did not put much stock in his words at first. They had heard it before. However, when Roosevelt forced two high ranking police officers to resign, they began to realize that he actually meant what he said.

Roosevelt soon became convinced that the most effective way of dismantling the corruption in the police department was by enforcing the law requiring that saloons be closed on Sundays. This law had been on the books for forty years; however, it had never been enforced. Rather, it "had warped into a massive vehicle of police and political blackmail."[74] Saloon owners and managers who made their monthly payments to Tammany remained open on Sunday. Those who did not make their payments were immediately shut down and arrested for violating the law.

Though Roosevelt did not agree with this law, he knew that as police commissioner he needed to enforce it. He also knew that when he did enforce it the backlash from both saloon owners and saloon patrons would be huge, as Sunday was the only day off for most of the working men in the city. Committed as he was to abolishing corruption in the police force, though, he began the strict enforcement of this law on June 23, 1895. By mid-August more than 95 percent of the saloons in New York City were closed on Sunday.

Backlash

Though Roosevelt was successful in this endeavor, the price he paid was huge. In addition to the verbal abuse he received in countless telegrams and newspaper articles, the mayor and Republican bosses all turned against him. The mayor hinted to him that he might be removed from his position if he didn't ease up on the enforcement of this law. Roosevelt refused to ease up and refused to resign. Then, in the November 1895 city election, all the Republican candidates lost to the Tammany candidates and the party bosses blamed Roosevelt. In addition, the three commissioners who served on the board with Roosevelt began to sabotage any more of his attempts to root out corruption in the police department.

As his work with the NYPD was effectively stalled, Roosevelt became involved in the 1896 presidential campaign. He campaigned tirelessly for the Republican presidential candidate, William McKinley. When McKinley was elected president, he appointed Roosevelt Assistant Secretary of the Navy. This gave Roosevelt an honorable way to exit the NYPD.

Roosevelt served as Assistant Secretary of the Navy until April 1898, when the United States and Spain declared war on each other. He then resigned to serve in the armed forces.

After leaving the army, he campaigned for governorship of New York in the 1898 election and won. Once again, true to form, Roosevelt took up his ongoing battle against robber barons and corrupt politicians in order to protect workers. During his tenure as governor, he was able to get legislation passed "establishing an eight-hour day for state employees, limiting the maximum hours women and children could work in private industry, improving working conditions for children, hiring more factory inspectors, and mandating air brakes on freight trains. At a time when laissez-faire attitudes reigned, even such limited measures represented considerable progress."[75]

He also fought a major battle against corporate monopolies, which practically consumed his governorship and had far-reaching implications and consequences. He initiated this battle by announcing his support of a new franchise tax on corporations. When he made this announcement, he experienced a head-on collision with Senator Thomas Platt, Republican Party boss.

Backdrop

For decades, the state of New York had granted exclusive franchises to corporations to operate immensely lucrative electric street railways, telephone networks, and telegraph lines. These franchises, often secured by outright bribery, had been awarded with no attempt to obtain tax revenues from the corporations in return. After investigating the issue, Roosevelt concluded "that it was a matter of plain decency" for these corporations to pay their share of taxes for privileges worth tens or even hundreds of millions."[76]

Twenty years earlier, every business had maintained its own lobby in Albany, an expensive and often inefficient way of influencing the state legislature. Platt made it his business "to bring order out of confusion," centralizing power in his own hands. He first persuaded corporations to contribute generously to the state central committee rather than field individual lobbyists, and then allocated the money to elect the machine's slate of candidates. Over time, Platt built up a majority of legislators absolutely beholden to his organization. Corporations thrived under the Platt regime; it cost less to support the state committee than to keep individual lobbies. Furthermore, since Platt took none of the money for himself, "there were no longer stories of individual corruption, of bribes and scandals." But the people of New York bore the cost of the system that worked so seamlessly for both the corporations and the politicians.[77]

To keep control of the political organization he required regular revenue from the corporate world "in the guise of contributions for campaign purposes" and donations for "the good of the party." These sums were distributed to his select candidates for the state legislature with the "gentleman's understanding" that they could be counted upon for important votes, particularly when an issue touched upon the corporations that fueled the machine. The public had small awareness and less understanding of this threat that Roosevelt labeled the "invisible empire."[78]

Through a complicated series of maneuvers, the bill was finally brought to a vote in both chambers just before the legislative session ended. While many Republicans in the lower chamber heeded Platt's directive to vote against the measure, Roosevelt secured enough Republican support that, combined with a heavy democratic vote, he was able to produce a majority.[79]

This resulted in Roosevelt coming under fierce attack by Platt and multiple corporate representatives, all of whom threatened that he would never again be nominated for public office if he signed the bill into law. Realizing that a break from the Republican Party would be the death knell for his political career, he agreed to some amendments to the bill that satisfied both Platt and the corporate representatives. Roosevelt then signed it into law.

Roosevelt's "struggle for the franchise tax had sensitized him to the 'growth of popular unrest and popular distrust' over the increasing concentration of power in large corporations," and he "consulted a variety of experts to develop a reasonable proposal for regulating the trusts."[80]

The trusts that Roosevelt referred to are corporate trusts, i.e., large businesses with significant market power, monopolies or near-monopolies.

It's important to remember that Roosevelt was not against trusts. He was against bad trusts. He was not out to destroy or abolish big business. He was out "to distinguish good trusts that yielded efficient operations, lower prices, and better service, from bad trusts that used predatory tactics to gain monopoly, artificially depress production, and extort unreasonable prices."[81] Roosevelt stated his position with utter clarity in a private letter to a journalist. He stated, "I believe in corporations. I believe in trade unions. Both have come to stay and are necessities in our present industrial system. But where, in either the one or the other, there develops corruption or mere brutal indifference to the rights of others . . . then the offender, whether union or corporation, must be fought."[82]

In an address to the New York Legislature, Roosevelt "insisted on the state's right to protect the public from monopoly and even from the 'colossal waste' of resources in 'vulgar forms of social advertisement.'" He went on to say that "with the facts in hand, measures—including taxation—could be devised to regulate the trusts."[83]

Following this address, his conflictual relationship with Platt and with Benjamin Odell, Chairman of the Republican State Committee, rose to a whole new level.

"Tensions with the party bosses escalated further when the governor threw his support behind a bill that would compel corporations to disclose information on their 'structure and finance.'"[84] That bill did not pass. "The dangers of the trusts, apparent to farmers and wage earners, had not yet penetrated the consciousness of middle-class America . . . the trusts remained amorphous entities, arousing vague apprehension but insufficient outrage to exert pressure on the political machines operating as their protectors. And in the absence of public demand, it was not difficult for Platt to prevent the legislature from acting on Roosevelt's proposal."[85]

In 1900, as William McKinley was preparing to run for a second term as president, the party bosses nominated Roosevelt to be his running mate. They did this to silence and paralyze him, as the vice-presidency is virtually an impotent position. In November 1900 Roosevelt stepped out of the position of governor of New York and accepted the vice-presidential nomination. McKinley won the election, and Roosevelt moved into the position of vice-president in March 1901. McKinley died in September 1901 as the result of a gunshot wound, and Roosevelt became president.

Backdrop

When Roosevelt became president, the Senate was controlled by Republicans who were allied with big business and their states' political machines. Senator Mark Hanna, known as the "national boss" of the Republican Party, had been able to successfully block all anti-trust legislation from being prosecuted in the two years prior to Roosevelt's presidential inauguration. One journalist described Hanna's operation as "the management of the American people in the interest of the American businessman for the profit of American business and politics."[86]

Roosevelt did not let any of this stop him. In his first message to Congress, he stated firmly that the trusts needed to be "supervised and within reasonable limits controlled."[87] He proposed the creation of a new Department of Commerce, whose function would be to monitor corporate finances in order to determine if regulation or taxation were necessary.

Much like the police department's reaction to his first press conference, the corporate world's reaction to his statements regarding monitoring corporate finances was to not take his words seriously. They were therefore stunned when two months later he "announced the government's intention to bring an anti-trust suit against the Northern Securities Company. This giant holding company had recently merged the rail and shipping lines of James Hill, J. P. Morgan, and Cornelius Vanderbilt in the Northwest with those of E. H. Harriman, the Rockefellers, and the Goulds in the Southwest."[88]

> For a quarter of a century, Roosevelt later observed, "the power of the mighty industrial overlords of the country had increased with giant strides, while the methods of controlling them, or checking abuses by them on the part of the people, through the Government, remained archaic and therefore practically impotent." The anti-trust suit "served notice on everybody that it was going to be the Government, and not the Harrimans, who governed these United States." At the same time, Roosevelt's actions clearly demonstrated to powerful Republican leaders "that he was President in fact as well as in name."[89]

He then focused his attention on the beef trust. "The advent of refrigerated freight cars had diminished the advantage once held by local butchers, facilitating consolidation among the big national firms."[90] This not only impacted the income of local butchers but also impacted the wallets of local consumers by dramatically increasing the price of meat. After thorough investigation by the Justice Department, Roosevelt decided to bring suit against the beef trust.

By December 1902 Congress had failed to take action regarding the trusts. The bill to establish a Department of Commerce with power to obtain information and make decisions regarding regulating corporate trusts had been effectively blocked by Republicans. So, in his second annual address to Congress on December 2, 1902, he again proposed the creation of a Department of Commerce with extensive power to monitor corporate trusts.

As Congress reconvened in the winter of 1903, "Republican leaders in the Senate spread the word that there would be 'no time for anti-trust legislation at this session.'"[91]

Roosevelt's reaction:

Summoning the leaders of both branches together, he threatened to exercise the president's constitutional power to call an extra session "on extraordinary occasions" unless his anti-trust proposals were brought to the floor before adjournment. "While I could not force anyone to vote for the bills," he explained to a friend, "I felt

I had a right to demand that there should be a vote upon them."[92]

The three proposals to be voted on were:

- Strengthening of existing laws against discriminatory railroad rebates.
- A bill to expedite legal proceedings against suspected trusts.
- Establishment of a cabinet-level Department of Commerce with regulatory powers over large corporations.

The proposals did get to the floor and did get voted on. The first two passed relatively quickly and easily. The third, however, encountered fierce opposition. Corporate leaders, particularly John D. Rockefeller, brought all their power and influence to bear in an attempt to defeat this bill. They were ultimately unsuccessful due to very wise strategic maneuvering by Roosevelt. Before that session of Congress ended, the Department of Commerce and Labor with a Bureau of Corporations was established.

The anti-trust suit against the Northern Securities Company that had been announced in December 1901 reached the Supreme Court in March 1904. The Court found in favor of the government on March 14, 1904. "Even as he savored his dramatic victory, Roosevelt nevertheless made clear that the government would not 'run amuck'. While the nation possessed the right and responsibility to regulate corporations, he maintained, 'this power should be exercised with extreme caution.'"[93]

In November 1904 Roosevelt was elected president in his own right. During his second term he took on Standard Oil, "the mother of all trusts."

Backstory

In 1904 oil fields were found in Kansas and Oklahoma.

> The Standard Oil Company immediately began furnishing tanks, building refineries, and constructing pipelines. Independent producers were placated with the promise that they would receive market price for their oil. Only when Standard had a total lock on refining and transportation . . . did the company "put on the screws." A barrel of oil that had yielded a dollar and eighteen cents in 1904 had dropped to thirty-seven cents a year later. With control of both in-state refineries and all the pipelines, Standard Oil had effectively become "the only transporter and buyer" of the region's crude oil, with power to set whatever price it chose . . . Congressman Philip Campbell of southeast Kansas introduced a resolution requesting an investigation into "the unusually large margin" between the price of Kansas crude oil and the market price of refined products.[94]

In February 1905 Roosevelt directed Bureau of Corporations director James Garfield to thoroughly investigate Standard Oil's method of operation. Garfield "traveled to 'nearly all of the great fields' and talked with hundreds of producers, refiners, and railroad men. Special agents were dispatched throughout the United States and even to Europe."[95]

Garfield's report revealed that Standard Oil received "rebates, bribes, and kickbacks" from the railroads, which "had facilitated development of the trust's extensive pipeline system." The report also "outlined the monopolistic position of Standard Oil in the petroleum industry."[96]

The government charged Standard of Indiana with receiving illegal rebates from the Chicago & Alton Railroad. Standard was subsequently found guilty and fined $29,240,000. One year later an appeals court judge overturned the decision on a technicality. Six months after that the attorney general filed suit in St. Louis, charging Standard Oil of New Jersey and its five dozen subsidiaries with conspiracy to monopolize the oil industry in violation of the Sherman Anti-Trust Act . . . The federal court found in the government's favor. Two years later . . . the Supreme Court affirmed the lower court's ruling. The High Court condemned Standard Oil, "not because it is a trust, but because it has an infamous record." . . . Standard Oil was given six months to dissolve . . . Standard Oil of New Jersey eventually morphed into Exxon; Standard Oil of New York incorporated as Mobil; and Standard Oil of Indiana evolved into Amoco.[97]

In 1906 Roosevelt's suit against the beef trust, which had been initiated in 1902, finally took center stage. The publication of Upton Sinclair's novel *The Jungle*, which shone a spotlight on the beef trust, was the catalyst for bringing it to the stage. The novel was set in Packingtown, the stockyard district of Chicago. Though the characters in the book were fictitious, the setting was real, and the story was similar, if not identical, to those of many real people.

In April 1906 Roosevelt, after reading the book, ordered an investigation of the stockyards to evaluate the authenticity of Sinclair's descriptions.

> Roosevelt's inspectors found stockyard conditions comparable to those Sinclair had portrayed . . . These findings were more than sufficient to convince Roosevelt to take action. On May 22, Illinois senator Albert Beveridge introduced a White House-backed bill to institute a rigid federal inspection program covering all phases of the meatpacking industry, from animal slaughter to sausage and canned meat production. If products were "found healthful and fit for human food," a government label indicating "inspected and passed" would be attached; if not, the meat products would be marked "inspected and condemned." Roosevelt warned Senate leaders friendly to the packers "that unless effective meat inspection legislation were enacted without loss of time," he would make the report public. Although he had no desire to harm the packing industry or the livestock producers, if the meatpackers moved to kill the legislation, he would feel compelled to expose the sickening work conditions. Fearing adverse publicity even more than regulation, the packers retreated. Without a "dissenting vote" the Beveridge bill passed the Senate three days after it was introduced . . . The

legislation, meanwhile, foundered in the House Agricultural Committee, chaired by the wealthy stockbreeder James Wadsworth, a strong proponent of the beef trust . . . A series of emasculating amendments was prepared, one negating the "mandatory character" of inspection and granting packers the right of court review. "I am sorry to have to say," Roosevelt informed Congressman Wadsworth, "that it seems to me that each change is for the worse and that in the aggregate they are ruinous, taking away every particle of good from the suggested Beveridge amendment." Because the packers and their representatives had reneged, producing only "sham" legislation, the president felt he was not "warranted" any longer in holding back the report."[98]

Roosevelt then released a portion of the report to the press and put Congress on notice that if federal legislation were not passed, the entire report would be released. Congress did eventually pass a satisfactory bill regulating the beef trust.

In closing

Though Roosevelt addressed many other issues and concerns, both domestic and international, while he was president, I have singled out the actions he took to protect workers to underscore the fact that once he had implemented his second course correction, thereby changing his definition of success, he never wavered. He remained committed to improving conditions for workers while holding accountable those who employed corrupt practices in order to increase their own wealth and power, irrespective of the cost to the workers who labored to give them that wealth and power. Once he loosened "the 'steel chain' of conservative opposition to government intervention in the economic and social processes that had been his birthright,"[99] he never tightened it again, thus earning himself the nickname "the great trust buster."

Roosevelt lived as a private citizen from 1909 until his death on January 5, 1919. He died in his sleep as the result of a blood clot detaching from a vein and traveling to his lungs.

CHAPTER FIVE

PURPOSE: A CALLING

Purpose is radically different from success. The most significant difference is the starting point. When developing our definition of success, the starting point is ourselves. When attempting to discern our purpose, the starting point is God.

We choose our definition of success, either consciously or unconsciously, and we choose how to measure success; we do not choose our purpose. God chooses our purpose and then calls us to it. Though we don't choose our purpose, we do choose whether to respond to God's call and fulfill the purpose he chose for us.

An abundant life

"'I came that they may have life, and have it abundantly'" (John 10:10 RSV). Jesus spoke these words after he had given sight to a man who had been born blind. It seems apparent from these words that Jesus doesn't want us to live a mediocre life, i.e., a life characterized by mere comfort, or worse, boredom or pain or fear or depression or frustration. He doesn't want us to live in survival mode, just making it, just getting by day by day. He wants us to live abundant lives.

Important Note: The abundance that Jesus referred to is not financial or material abundance. It is an abundance of *life*. He wants us to live a life in which we are happy, fulfilled, energized, and passionate.

He also wants us to live a life of peace. This peace is not an external peace in relationships, communities, countries, or the world. It is an unshakeable internal peace that lives below our feelings and does not change when circumstances change. During the last meal he shared with the apostles before his crucifixion, he told them, "'I am leaving you with a gift—peace of mind and heart. And the peace I give is a gift the world cannot give. So don't be troubled or afraid'" (John 14:27). As the meal was ending, he said, "'I have told you all this so that you may have peace in me. Here on earth you will have many trials and sorrows. But take heart, because I have overcome the world'" (John 16:33).

Note: Jesus did not tell them that their external lives would be peaceful. He told them that they would have many trials and sorrows. He also told them that their peace would be *in him*. So, when we trust Jesus and keep our eyes (our spiritual eyes) on him, we will have internal peace regardless of what is going on in our external world.

How do we obtain this peace? By fulfilling God's purpose for our lives.

God has a plan

The concept of God having a plan and a purpose for each individual he creates is referenced throughout the Bible. Isaiah and Jeremiah were two Old Testament prophets who believed that God has a purpose and a plan for everyone. (A prophet is someone whom God chooses to be his mouthpiece on earth. God gives messages to his prophets, and the prophets then relay the messages to the people God designates.)

Isaiah told Cyrus, a pagan king, about God's purposes and plans for him. Speaking for God, Isaiah told Cyrus, "And why have I called you for this work? Why did I call you by name when you did not know me? It is for the sake of Jacob my servant, Israel my chosen one. I am the LORD; there is no other God. I have equipped you for battle, though you don't even know me" (Isaiah 45:4–5).

The people of Israel then began to question God for working through a pagan king. To them, Isaiah said,

> What sorrow awaits those who argue with
> their Creator.
> Does a clay pot argue with its maker?
> Does the clay dispute with the one who
> shapes it, saying,
> "Stop, you're doing it wrong!"
> Does the pot exclaim,
> "How clumsy can you be!"
> How terrible it would be if a newborn baby
> said to its father,
> "Why was I born?"

or if it said to its mother,
"Why did you make me this way?"

This is what the LORD says—
the Holy One of Israel and your Creator:
"Do you question what I do for my children?
Do you give me orders about the work of
        my hands?
I am the one who made the earth
and created people to live on it.
With my hands I stretched out the heavens.
All the stars are at my command.
I will raise up Cyrus to fulfill my righteous
        purpose,
and I will guide his actions." (Isaiah 45:9–13)

Isaiah was telling the people of Israel in no uncertain terms that God is sovereign, that he knows what he is doing, and that he chooses whoever he wants to do whatever he wants.

In a letter to the Israelites who were in exile in Babylon, Jeremiah told them, "'For I know the plans I have for you,' says the LORD. 'They are plans for good and not for disaster, to give you a future and a hope'" (Jeremiah 29:11).

A New Testament figure who believed that God has a specific purpose for everyone he creates, and who had a very clear understanding, as well as acceptance, of the role God wanted him to play, was John the Baptist.

At this time, John the Baptist was baptizing
at Aenon, near Salim . . . John's disciples came

to him and said, "Rabbi, the man you met on the other side of the Jordan River, the one you identified as the Messiah, is also baptizing people. And everybody is going to him instead of coming to us."

John replied, "No one can receive anything unless God gives it from heaven. You yourselves know how plainly I told you, "I am not the Messiah. I am only here to prepare the way for him." (John 3:23, 26–28)

The apostle Paul also believed this. In his letter to the church in Corinth, he stated, "We will not boast about things done outside our area of authority. We will boast only about what has happened within the boundaries of the work God has given us" (2 Corinthians 10:13).

Rick Warren, a modern-day spiritual leader, says, "Before God created you, he decided what role he wanted you to play on earth. He planned exactly how he wanted you to serve him, and then he shaped you for those tasks. You are the way you are because you were made for a specific ministry."[100]

My journey to purpose

As for myself, I have always believed that God exists and that he created me. Beginning at a young age, I was taught this in Catholic Church and in Catholic school, and I never questioned it or doubted it. It was several decades, however, before I understood and believed that God loves me and has a plan for me.

Early in my faith walk (mid to late 1990s), I started experiencing a nagging sense that I was supposed to do something for God. It kept gnawing at me inside and wouldn't go away. Though I had this feeling that I was supposed to do something for God, I didn't have the faintest idea what it was I was supposed to do. In an effort to try to understand what it was God wanted me to do, I served on and then led a committee in my church and also served in a number of different ministries. Though each of these was good and enjoyable and somewhat fulfilling, not one of them felt like the right fit. While serving in each one I felt as though I was wearing a jacket with shoulders that were too tight and sleeves that were too short.

In 2003 God finally let me know what he wanted me to do. I was leading a group in the church's Small Group Ministry when a notice went out to all the small group leaders that the senior pastor was going to Saddleback Church in California to learn about a faith-based recovery program called Celebrate Recovery. The notice included an open invitation for anyone who was interested to join him. I went, and while I was there God finally let me know what he wanted me to do for him. He convinced me beyond the shadow of a doubt that he wanted me to lead a Celebrate Recovery ministry at my church. When we got back to Pennsylvania, the church did decide to start a Celebrate Recovery ministry, and I did become the ministry leader.

You would think that once someone understands God's purpose for her life and begins to walk out that purpose, all would be clear sailing. Nothing could be further from the truth. Establishing and leading the Celebrate Recovery ministry was far harder than I had ever imagined it would be. It was one of the most difficult years of my life. It was full of struggle, challenges, conflict, anger, hurt, fear, and self-doubt. Power battles abounded. My leadership was constantly challenged and undermined.

There was a period of time in spring '04 during which I was particularly discouraged and full of doubt. One morning while I was praying, I asked God to show me what I needed to read or needed to hear, and I opened my Bible. It opened to 1 Chronicles 28 (David commissioning Solomon to build the Temple). I started to read that chapter, and the last two verses almost jumped off the page at me:

> Then David continued, "Be strong and courageous, and do the work. Don't be afraid or discouraged, for the Lord God, my God, is with you. He will not fail you or forsake you. He will see to it that all the work related to the Temple of the Lord is finished correctly. The various divisions of priests and Levites will serve in the Temple of God. Others with skills of every kind will volunteer, and the officials and the entire nation are at your command." (1 Chronicles 28:20–21)

This confirmed to me that God did indeed want me to be a leader. I began to read those verses every day, sometimes multiple times in one day, and I slowly began to feel the burden of weight lifted off my shoulders. I *knew* that I wasn't alone, that God was in control. All I had to do was follow his plan, and he would do the rest. As I trusted that more and more, my faith became stronger, my fear decreased, and I began to lead with a greater degree of confidence and purpose.

As I look back and reflect on this time in my life, I believe God gave me the Celebrate Recovery ministry to lead in order to break my spirit of independence. The ministry was too big to lead using my own abilities as I had historically done with everything else. He put me in a position where I had to depend on him and his power.

In August 2004 I went back to Saddleback Church for the 2004 Celebrate Recovery Summit. The passion and the commitment to Celebrate Recovery emanating from everyone there was the same as it had been the previous year. I knew I was home. The inner peace and the sense of belonging I experienced were profound. I knew I had finally found the exact right fit.

As I continued to lead the Celebrate Recovery ministry at my home church, I knew I was walking in the will of God for my life. I knew who God had created me to be, and I not only felt good about it—I rejoiced in it. This knowing was accompanied by a profound inner peace and joy that were unlike anything I had ever experienced. Based on this experience, I developed my own definition of success, i.e., "Success is faithfully walking the path carved out for you by God, fulfilling his purpose for your life." My measure of success, which flows naturally from my definition of success, will be to hear, when I stand before God, "Well done, good and faithful servant."

Though I was experiencing an internal peace and joy that could only have come from God, the external opposition continued unabated. As I truly led the ministry, the challenges to my leadership and the power struggles intensified, until they culminated in a head-on collision with the stained-glass ceiling.

Note: The stained-glass ceiling is a metaphor "indicating a certain level of power and authority within church structures that women tend not to rise above within church hierarchies" (Wikipedia). It is patterned after the glass ceiling metaphor that has long been used in the corporate world to describe the invisible, yet real, limit placed on women trying to climb the corporate ladder.

In his worship song "Blessed Be Your Name," Matt Redman sings, "He gives and takes away." Those words came alive for me in November 2004 when the leadership of Celebrate Recovery was taken away from me by the pastors and some other leaders in the church. I didn't see it coming, and I was initially in shock. When the shock lessened, I was devastated. I spent the next two years wandering in the wilderness, lost. I began a period of deep grieving and mourning. I was hurt, angry, depressed. I felt as though I was wandering in the wilderness, lost, so I went to a Celebrate Recovery program at another church to heal my wounds.

Lessons

I've heard it said that great lessons are learned in times of great pain, and that certainly proved to be true for me during my time in the wilderness. It's difficult to describe the depth of joy I felt at discovering and fulfilling God's purpose for my life. It's even more difficult to describe the depth of pain I felt at having it ripped away from me by human beings.

Though I was in more emotional pain than at almost any other time in my life, I did not see my removal from my leadership position in the Celebrate Recovery ministry as a God thing. I saw it as a human thing. At the same time, I also believed that it could not have happened unless God allowed it to happen. In Rick Warren's words, "Regardless of the cause, none of your problems could happen without God's permission. Everything that happens to a child of God is Father-filtered, and he intends to use it for good even when Satan and others mean it for bad."[101]

The good that came out of this is that, during my time in the wilderness, God taught me to trust him and his timing and his plan on a much deeper level. He taught me to truly wait on him. "But those who wait upon GOD get fresh strength. They spread their wings and soar like eagles, they run and don't get tired, they walk and don't lag behind" (Isaiah 40:31 MSG).

He also taught me to forgive. My healing process moved along in fits and starts. I experienced victories followed by relapses. As this happened repeatedly, I came to understand that God had a very special purpose for this time in my life. I gradually realized that, just as he had given me the Celebrate Recovery ministry to lead in order to break my spirit of independence, he allowed it to be taken away from me so he could teach me to forgive. He slowly and convincingly showed me my spirit of unforgiveness. I came to see that my life was not characterized by forgiveness, as Jesus wants his followers' lives to be. Rather, my life was characterized by holding grudges and harboring bitterness, resentment, and a desire for vengeance.

As this realization took root in me, I began to study forgiveness. I came across a definition of forgiveness in Lewis B. Smedes's book *The Art of Forgiving*. That definition is: "Forgiving . . . is an art, a practical art, maybe the most neglected of all the healing arts. It is the art of healing inner wounds inflicted by other people's wrongs."[102] As I continued to study forgiveness, I learned what forgiveness is and what it is not.

I learned that forgiveness is:

- A choice—I don't have to feel like forgiving someone in order to forgive him or her.
- A free gift given with no strings attached.
- Surrendering our right to get even.
- Choosing to keep no record of the wrongs.
- Being merciful.
- Being gracious.
- Letting go of bitterness.
- A heart condition—forgiveness takes place in the forgiver's heart. It is intrapersonal, not interpersonal.
- A permanent condition, a lifelong commitment—I cannot forgive someone and take it back later.

I learned that forgiveness is not:

- Forgetting.
- Excusing the wrong that was done.
- Tolerating the wrong that was done.
- Denying the wrong that was done.

- Justifying what was done.
- Refusing to take the wrong seriously.
- Pretending that we are not hurt.
- Erasing the need for consequences.
- Quick.
- Easy.
- A magic balm that takes away feelings of hurt and anger.

Though all of the above lessons I learned about forgiveness were important, the most important ones were:

- The choice whether or not to forgive does not depend on the wrongdoer's attitude or perception of the wrong—I can choose to forgive someone whether or not they see themselves as having done something wrong, and whether or not they are sorry.
- Forgiveness is not the same as reconciliation—I can forgive someone and choose not to re-enter into a relationship with him or her.
- Forgiveness is an essential, non-negotiable ingredient in the healing of deep wounds. In these instances, forgiving benefits the forgiver far more than the forgiven.

As I struggled to forgive the pastors and other church leaders who had removed me from the leadership role of the Celebrate Recovery ministry, I fought against my desire to get back at them, to make them hurt as much as they had hurt me. During this process I was comforted by the following words in Smedes's book *Forgive & Forget, Healing the Hurts We Don't Deserve*: "Nobody seems to be born with much talent for forgiving. We all need to learn from scratch, and the learning almost always runs against the grain."[103]

As I continued to struggle and work on forgiving those who had hurt me, I quickly realized that I could not do it on my own. My desire for vengeance and payback was too strong. I needed God's help, his power. I began to daily ask God to give me an attitude and lifestyle of forgiveness. I simultaneously decided that I was no longer going to allow those pastors and leaders to steal my joy. They had already taken too much from me, and I was not going to allow them to take anything more. As I daily prayed this prayer and reiterated my decision, my peace and joy slowly came back, and I was finally able to exit the wilderness.

Over the next seven years I served in leadership roles in two Celebrate Recovery ministries near my home. Then, in 2013, I started reaping what I had sown and harvesting what I had planted. The consequences of a lifetime of failing to take care of my physical body caught up with me. Some medical problems that I had been ignoring could no longer be ignored. I stepped out of the leadership role I was serving in at that time and over the next year underwent two major surgeries. I spent that year healing physically, as well as replenishing emotionally and spiritually. While doing so, God let me know that I was no longer to serve in the Celebrate Recovery ministry. That season of my life was over.

New assignment

In July 2014 God lit a fire in my heart to set his daughters free from the belief systems and practices that reinforce the inequality of the sexes.

When God first gave me that directive, I wondered why he had chosen *me*, an outspoken woman who had been raised in the suburbs of New York City in a liberal Irish Catholic Democratic family and who was currently living in Lancaster, Pennsylvania, to do this. I wondered whether God had a sense of humor and if watching me try to walk out this purpose in Lancaster County (one of the most, if not *the* most, traditional, conservative counties in the United States) would entertain him. I slowly came to realize, though, that as the civil rights battle was fought in the South, where racism was the most blatant, the gender equality battle needs to be fought here, one of the major strongholds of gender inequality. As he has not given me a platform from which to advocate for gender equality, I plant seeds for it, one person at a time.

The following parable Jesus told one day to a crowd who had gathered around him is now the rudder that guides my actions.

> A farmer went out to plant some seeds. As he scattered them across his field, some seeds fell on a footpath, and the birds came and ate them. Other seeds fell on shallow soil with underlying rock. The seeds sprouted quickly because the soil was shallow. But the plants soon wilted under the hot sun, and since they didn't have deep roots,

they died. Other seeds fell among thorns that grew up and choked out the tender plants. Still other seeds fell on fertile soil, and they produced a crop that was thirty, sixty, and even a hundred times as much as had been planted! . . .

Now listen to the explanation of the parable about the farmer planting seeds: The seed that fell on the footpath represents those who hear the message about the Kingdom and don't understand it. Then the evil one comes and snatches away the seed that was planted in their hearts. The seed on the rocky soil represents those who hear the message and immediately receive it with joy. But since they don't have deep roots, they don't last long. They fall away as soon as they have problems or are persecuted for believing God's word. The seed that fell among the thorns represents those who hear God's word, but all too quickly the message is crowded out by the worries of this life and the lure of wealth, so no fruit is produced. The seed that fell on good soil represents those who truly hear and understand God's word and produce a harvest of thirty, sixty, or even a hundred times as much as had been planted! (Matthew 13:3–8, 18–23)

I am now planting seeds for gender equality, one person at a time. Whether or not those seeds sprout a single plant, a harvest of plants, or no plants at all is outside my control. My responsibility is to plant the seed. What happens from there is up to the individual and to God.

The other side

There is another side to this whole concept of fulfilling God's purpose for our lives. That is, we are not the only ones who lose when we fail to discover and fulfill our purpose. Due to the system of human interdependence that God designed, everything we do or fail to do affects others. By not discovering and fulfilling God's plan for us, we not only miss experiencing the peace and joy that only God can give, but others miss out as well. As Rick Warren states,

> God designed each of us so there would be no duplication in the world. No one has the exact same mix of factors that make you unique. That means no one else on earth will ever be able to play the role God planned for you. If you don't make your unique contribution to the Body of Christ, it won't be made.[104]

CHAPTER SIX

OBEDIENCE: THE PATHWAY TO PURPOSE

"If you do not carry your own cross and follow me, you cannot be by disciple" (Luke 14:27). "In carrying that cross, we find liberty and joy and fulfillment."[105]

Carrying your own cross means being obedient to God, fulfilling the purpose he chose especially for you. Jesus came to earth to die on a cross. That was his purpose. As discussed in the previous chapter, God also put each of us on earth to fulfill a specific purpose that he chose for us and designed us to fulfill. Whether or not we fulfill it, i.e., carry our cross, is our choice. It is in carrying that cross, however, that we become fully who God created us to be. When we become who God created us to be and do what God created us to do, we experience an unshakeable internal peace and joy that is beyond human understanding or attainment. It is the peace and joy that can come only from God. It lives below our feelings and does not change when our circumstances change. There is a price for this peace and joy, however. The price is obedience. The payoff is freedom, spiritual freedom, resurrection style freedom.

Obedience, submission, and *surrender* are not popular words in our culture. We tend to want to do what we want to do, when we want to do it, and how we want to do it. Submitting to another's authority is not always welcome or desirable or easy. Submitting to God's authority for our life, however, and obeying his will for us, is the pathway to purpose—the only pathway to purpose.

Those of us who are human parents want many things for and from our children. One of the main things we want from our children is obedience, unquestioning obedience without discussion, negotiation, argument, and so forth. I doubt there is a human parent alive who has not used the phrase "Because I said so!" when trying to get children to do something. The same holds true for God, our Heavenly Parent. From the beginning of creation God gave much to his children, and all he asked for in return was obedience. His children, right from the beginning, had a difficult time giving this to him.

Comic relief

After creating heaven and earth God created Adam and Eve and the first thing he said was "Don't!"

"Don't what?" Adam replied.

"Don't eat the forbidden fruit" God said.

"Forbidden fruit? We have forbidden fruit? Hey Eve, we have forbidden fruit!"

"No way!"

"Yes way."

"DO NOT eat the fruit!" God said.

"Why?!"

"Because I'm your Father and I said so!" God replied, wondering why he hadn't stopped creation after making the elephants.

A few minutes later God saw his children taking an apple break and was he ticked!

"Didn't I tell you not to eat the fruit?" God, our first parent, asked.

"Uh huh," Adam replied.

"Then why did you?" asked God.

"I don't know," said Eve.

"She started it!" said Adam.

"Did not!"

"Did too!"

"DID NOT!"

Having had it with the two of them God's punishment was that Adam and Eve have children of their own. Thus, the pattern was set, and it has never changed. (Author Unknown)

On a serious note, I am not advocating blind obedience to God. I am advocating a conscious decision to submit to his authority for your life after you have gotten to know him and learned to trust him. God gave each of us free will, and he wants us to use our free will when deciding to become part of his family. He doesn't want mindless puppets obeying him because they were taught to do so as children. He wants people to freely choose to obey him because they love him, trust him, are grateful to him, and fear him with a biblical fear.

Important Note: Biblical fear of God is not the same as being afraid that we'll be hurt or scared of a harsh punishment. That is worldly fear. Biblical fear is more like awe or respect. God himself spoke of this kind of fear through Jeremiah. "Have you no respect for me? Why don't you tremble in my presence?" (Jeremiah 5:22). The writer of the book of Acts also spoke of this kind of fear when he said: "The story of what happened spread quickly all through Ephesus, to Jews and Greeks alike. A solemn fear descended on the city, and the name of the Lord Jesus was greatly honored" (Acts 19:17). So, if one fears God with a biblical fear, one is in awe of God. One respects and honors him. If one fears God with a worldly fear, one is afraid that God will mete out harsh punishment and/ or withdraw his love.

An Old Testament figure who loved God, trusted him, and feared him with a biblical fear was Noah. Due to this love, trust, and fear, Noah obeyed God without question.

Backstory

After Adam and Eve left the Garden of Eden, the human race grew and multiplied and eventually became quite evil. Noah was the only person who did not do evil in God's sight. God therefore told Noah that he was going to destroy the human race with a great flood. God then told Noah to build a boat, and Noah built a boat.

Interesting fact: When God told Noah to build this boat, Noah was in the middle of a desert!

Can you imagine how ridiculous it must have seemed to Noah's neighbors that he was building a boat? Can you also imagine how much grief Noah and his family probably took because he was building this boat? Yet Noah did not let anything deter him. He obeyed God and built the boat, and, due to his unquestioning obedience, he and his family survived the flood.

God wants this same kind of obedience from us. He wants us to obey him without question, even when it seems to make no sense at all, *especially* when it makes no sense at all. He wants us to obey him because we know him, love him, trust him, and fear him with biblical fear. He does not want us to fear him with a worldly fear.

Another example of people obeying God out of biblical fear is how the Israelites obeyed him following their exodus from Egypt.

Backstory #2

After the flood the human race once again grew and multiplied. God eventually created a people who were set apart to belong to him, to be his family. He chose Abraham to be the father of his family and gave Abraham a vision of what would happen to his descendants long after his death. "God said to Abram, 'Know this: your descendants will live as outsiders in a land not theirs; they'll be enslaved and beaten down for 400 years. Then I'll punish their slave masters; your offspring will march out of there loaded with plunder'" (Genesis15:13–14 MSG).

The land "not theirs" that Abraham's descendants would end up in was Egypt. When God was ready to bring his family, the Israelites, out of slavery in Egypt, God chose Moses to lead them.

When the Israelites left Egypt under Moses's leadership, "The Lord went ahead of them. He guided them during the day with a pillar of cloud, and he provided light at night with a pillar of fire. This allowed them to travel by day or by night. And the Lord did not remove the pillar of cloud or pillar of fire from its place in front of the people" (Exodus 13:21–22).

> This was the regular pattern—at night the cloud that covered the Tabernacle had the appearance of fire. Whenever the cloud lifted from over the sacred tent, the people of Israel would break camp and follow it. And wherever the cloud settled, the people of Israel would set up camp. In this way, they traveled and camped at the Lord's command wherever he told them to go. Then they remained in their camp as long as the cloud stayed over the Tabernacle. If the cloud remained over the Tabernacle for a long time, the Israelites stayed and performed their duty to the Lord. Sometimes the cloud would stay over the Tabernacle for only a few days, so the people would stay for only a few days, as the Lord commanded. Then at the Lord's command they would break camp and move on. Sometimes the cloud stayed only overnight and lifted the next morning. But day or night, when the cloud lifted, the people broke camp and moved on.

Whether the cloud stayed above the Tabernacle for two days, a month, or a year, the people of Israel stayed in camp and did not move on. But as soon as it lifted, they broke camp and moved on. So they camped or traveled at the LORD's command, and they did whatever the LORD told them through Moses. (Numbers 9:16–23)

Whenever I read the account of how God guided the Israelites with the pillar of cloud and the pillar of fire after they left Egypt, I am impressed by how the people obeyed him. When the cloud lifted, the Israelites moved. When the cloud settled, they camped where it settled. When the cloud lifted again, they moved again. They didn't argue or try to move prematurely or try to set up camp somewhere else. They just followed the guidance of the Lord. They obeyed him. This made God smile, and he released his blessings, his provisions, on them. He took care of them. He made sure the Israelites had quail and bread and water so they wouldn't die of thirst or starvation.

In order for the Israelites to obey God so unquestioningly, they surely must have known him, trusted him, and loved him. "When you come to a moment of truth when you must choose whether to obey God, you cannot obey Him unless you believe and trust Him. You cannot believe and trust Him, unless you love Him. You cannot love Him, unless you know Him."[106]

§ Getting to know him

If one is to willingly agree to obey God, one first has to know God, the *real* God, not a distorted image of God. The real God is love. He doesn't merely have love. He doesn't just show love. He *is* love. It's his character. The apostle John explained this in one of the letters he wrote to the early church: "God is love, and all who live in love live in God, and God lives in them" (1 John 4:16).

Centuries before John wrote these words, King David spoke about God's character: "The LORD is compassionate and merciful, slow to get angry and filled with unfailing love . . . For his unfailing love toward those who fear him is as great as the height of the heavens above the earth . . . The LORD is like a father to his children, tender and compassionate to those who fear him" (Psalm 103: 8, 11, 13).

Though he loves us with a perfect love, he does not always give us everything we want or let us get away with bad behavior. Like any good parent, he gives his children what they *need*, not necessarily what they want. Sometimes he says no to us, sometimes he lets us experience the consequences of our choices and actions, and sometimes he disciplines us when we disobey him. He doesn't discipline us because he's angry at us or disappointed in us; he disciplines us because he loves us.

God's discipline

The word *discipline* comes from the same root as *disciple*, one who is taught. The goal of discipline is not to punish— it's to teach. True discipline has two purposes: education and behavior change. Punishment is a penalty, a consequence for breaking a law or a rule. The goal of punishment is to get people to the point where they will follow the rules or obey the law.

When God is disciplining us, he is trying to teach us to be more like his Son. He is trying to get us to the point where we will willingly replace sinful behavior with godly behavior. During these times of disciplining, we would be well advised to cooperate with the work God is doing in us and accept the disciplining process. The following words of Moses to the people of Israel hold true for us today as well: "Think about it: Just as a parent disciplines a child, the LORD your God disciplines you for your own good" (Deuteronomy 8:5). It all comes back to knowing God and trusting that everything he does, he does out of love.

If you have a hard time thinking of God as loving, think about Jesus. After all, Jesus was God with flesh on. Five days before his death Jesus said the following words to a crowd in Jerusalem: "'If you trust me, you are trusting not only me, but also God who sent me. For when you see me, you are seeing the one who sent me'" (John 12:44-45).

Then think about what Jesus did for us. He left the glory of heaven to take on human form and do something for us that we were not able to do for ourselves. He created the way for us to get to heaven. He explained this to his disciple Nathanael, "'I tell you the truth, you will all see heaven open and the angels of God going up and down on the Son of Man, the one who is the stairway between heaven and earth'" (John 1:51).

Love, not nails

When I reflect on what Jesus did for us that day at Calvary, I marvel at the choice he made. Jesus did not have to stay hanging on that cross; he *chose* to stay hanging there. Nails did not hold him to that cross—love held him to the cross, love for each and every one of us, past, present, and future. What Jesus did on the cross was the epitome of selfless love; i.e., he chose to do something for someone else regardless of the cost to himself.

If you want a picture of pure, perfect love, picture Jesus, bloody and beaten beyond recognition, hanging on a wooden cross. Jesus's action of staying nailed to that cross until he died was his gift of love for all people throughout time, including the people who crucified him and those who mocked and abused him as he hung on the cross.

> The people passing by shouted abuse, shaking their heads in mockery. "Look at you now!" they yelled at him. "You said you were going to destroy the Temple and rebuild it in three days. Well then, if you are the Son of God, save yourself and come down from the cross!"
>
> The leading priests, the teachers of religious law, and the elders also mocked Jesus. "He saved others," they scoffed, "but he can't save himself! So he is the King of Israel, is he? Let him come down from the cross right now, and we will believe in him! He trusted God, so let God rescue him now if he wants him! For he said, I am the Son of God." Even the revolutionaries who were

crucified with him ridiculed him in the same way." (Matthew 27:39–44)

What the leading priests, teachers of religious law, and elders didn't understand was that Jesus stayed on that cross for them. If Jesus had come down from the cross, which he was more than capable of doing, he would have saved himself. He would not, however, have saved them, and he would not have saved us.

To become part of God's family and spend eternity with him, we have to accept Jesus's gift of love. To accept his gift means that we believe Jesus truly was and is the Son of God and that he died for us, taking our place and paying the penalty for our sins and wrongdoings. There is nothing that we can do to earn this gift. It is a free gift that has already been given. The only choice we have is whether to accept it. The apostle Paul explained this to the church in Ephesus with the following words: "God saved you by his grace when you believed. And you can't take credit for this; it is a gift from God. Salvation is not a reward for the good things we have done, so none of us can boast about it" (Ephesians 2:8–9).

My journey to obedience

Growing up, I learned to see God as anything but loving. I learned that his love was conditional and that I had to earn his love through performing good works. I also learned to see him as a punishing God who was distant, critical, and judgmental and who didn't care about how I felt or what I needed. I was afraid of him with a worldly fear.

The process I went through to get to know the real God involved immersing myself in an extensive period of questioning, studying, and deciding what I believed and what I didn't believe. The result of this was that I finally began to understand that the real God is not the God I had learned about in my childhood. I began to believe that God really does love me and care about how I feel. I was realizing that God knows what I need and that he will take care of me and provide for me.

I spent months reading Matthew 6:25–33 (see Appendix 1) every day, and I slowly began to believe that if God takes care of the birds and the flowers, he will take care of me. I began to understand that he wants to be involved in my life day to day, minute to minute (not just for an hour on Sunday morning) and that he loves me so much that he sent his only Son, Jesus, to suffer and die for me and that Jesus would have suffered and died even if I were the only person on the planet!

I finally understood and believed that God wants me to have a relationship with Jesus and follow Jesus, not a bunch of man-made rules. I accepted the truth that there is nothing I could do to earn salvation, that it is a gift freely offered that I can either choose to accept or not accept. I chose to accept it and started my walk with Jesus.

As I walked with Jesus, I slowly began to realize that giving my life to him is not the same as surrendering my will to him. I began to understand that following Christ means seeking his guidance every second of every hour of every day. It is no longer about doing things my way; it is about choosing to do things his way. It is about putting him permanently in the driver's seat of my life.

Changing seats

I wish I could say that once I put Jesus in the driver's seat of my life, I left him there. Regrettably, that is not the case. There have been times when I put myself back in the driver's seat, doing life my way.

Growing up, I learned that other people's opinions were very important. I learned that their opinions were the source of my self-worth. I, of course, didn't realize at the time that I was learning these things; still, I grew into an approval seeker and people pleaser *par excellence*!

As I walked with Jesus, my understanding of where my worth came from slowly began to change. He taught me that my self-esteem and self-worth do not come from the approval of people. It comes from my relationship with him. I am a child of God, and therefore I have worth. As this truth took root in me, I began to see that the approval of human beings is unimportant and irrelevant. The only thing that is important is God's approval, which I already have by virtue of being his child.

Though I was living my life for an audience of One, at times I slipped back into my old pattern of seeking the approval of human beings to bolster my self-esteem. This would eventually blow up in my face, and I would remind myself that I no longer need to do that. As I am already assured of God's approval, I do not need the approval of human beings.

There have also been times that I did not obey him unquestioningly. For most of my adult life, including my first time serving in Celebrate Recovery, my time in the wilderness, and my early time serving in Celebrate Recovery post-wilderness, I worked as a mental health professional, a psychotherapist. At some point in mid to late 2006 God let me know that he wanted me to quit my job and leave the mental health field. Rather than obeying him and trusting him, however, I wrestled with him and tried to negotiate with him. He finally grew tired of my disobedience and wrestling and made it next to impossible for me to stay in my profession. So, in February 2008, I finally decided to obey him. I walked away from my career as a mental health professional and threw myself into the recovery ministry and into writing, the two things God wanted me to do.

When I allowed God to be in the driver's seat of my life, I experienced the peace and joy that can come only from God. When I put myself back in the driver's seat of my life, I was looking for that peace and joy to come from human achievements and human relationships. What I received were the peace and joy that the world gives. Having experienced both scenarios, I can tell you that the peace and joy that the world gives are hollow compared to the peace and joy that God gives. Nothing can compare to that deep certainty you feel when you know you are right where you are supposed to be, doing exactly what you were created to do.

God's choices

As stated above, God chooses whomever he wants to do whatever he wants. He chose two very unlikely candidates, an uneducated fisherman and an educated Pharisee, to be the two most influential leaders of the early church, and he prepared each of them to fulfill his unique calling. Nothing God does is random.

CHAPTER SEVEN

PETER'S STORY

Peter was among the first, if not *the* first, disciple of Jesus Christ. He got to know Jesus, learned to trust him, and eventually did what he was created to do.

Peter grew up in Bethsaida, a small fishing village on the banks of the Jordan River, in a Jewish family who practiced strict obedience of the Jewish law. When Peter met Jesus he lived in Capernaum, on the shores of the Sea of Galilee, and worked as a fisherman with his brother Andrew.

Note: Fishing in the first century was extremely demanding physically, quite unlike fishing in the twenty-first century. First-century fishermen were tough, strong, unkempt, shabbily dressed, and often used vulgar language. They must also have been somewhat fearless because unbelievably strong storms tended to come up on the Sea of Galilee quickly and unexpectedly. These storms could easily capsize the fishermen's boats.

Andrew introduced Peter to Jesus at a site on the Jordan River where John the Baptist was preaching. Jesus had traveled there from Nazareth to hear his cousin John preach. Peter had traveled to this same spot with Andrew and two other fishermen, Philip and Nathanael, to hear John preach.

> The following day John was again standing with two of his disciples. As Jesus walked by, John looked at him and declared, "Look, there is the Lamb of God!" When John's two disciples heard this, they followed Jesus.
>
> Jesus looked around and saw them following. "What do you want"? he asked them.
>
> They replied, "Rabbi" (which means "Teacher"), "where are you staying?"
>
> "Come and see," he said. It was about four o'clock in the afternoon when they went with him to the place where he was staying, and they remained with him the rest of the day.
>
> Andrew, Simon Peter's brother, was one of these men who heard what John said and then followed Jesus. Andrew went to find his brother, Simon, and told him, "We have found the Messiah" (which means "Christ").
>
> Then Andrew brought Simon to meet Jesus. Looking intently at Simon, Jesus said, "Your name is Simon, son of John—but you will be called Cephas" (which means "Peter"). (John 1:35–42)

Following this encounter, Peter returned to his life in Capernaum. He met Jesus again approximately a month and a half later. Following that second meeting, Peter became a disciple of Jesus.

Note: "To be a disciple of Jesus meant something more than being a student of a teacher. To be a disciple meant 'to follow after.' 'Whoever would be my disciple,' Jesus said, 'let him follow me.' What does it mean to be a follower of Jesus? It means to take seriously what he took seriously, to be like him in some sense."[107]

There are varying accounts as to how Peter decided to become a disciple of Jesus. Mark's and Matthew's accounts are virtually identical. "One day as Jesus was walking along the shore of the Sea of Galilee, he saw two brothers— Simon, also called Peter, and Andrew—throwing a net into the water, for they fished for a living. Jesus called out to them, 'Come, follow me, and I will show you how to fish for people!' And they left their nets at once and followed him" (Matthew 4:18–20). Luke recounts the same event; however, he expands the story, including much more detail.

> One day as Jesus was preaching on the shore of the Sea of Galilee, great crowds pressed in on him to listen to the word of God. He noticed two empty boats at the water's edge, for the fishermen had left them and were washing their nets. Stepping into one of the boats, Jesus asked Simon, its owner, to push it out into the water. So he sat in the boat and taught the crowds from there.
>
> When he had finished speaking, he said to Simon, "Now go out where it is deeper, and let down your nets to catch some fish."
>
> "Master," Simon replied, "we worked hard all last night and didn't catch a thing. But if you

say so, I'll let the nets down again." And this time their nets were so full of fish they began to tear! A shout for help brought their partners in the other boat, and soon both boats were filled with fish and on the verge of sinking.

When Simon Peter realized what had happened, he fell to his knees before Jesus and said, "Oh, Lord, please leave me—I'm too much of a sinner to be around you." For he was awestruck by the number of fish they had caught, as were the others with him. His partners, James and John, the sons of Zebedee, were also amazed.

Jesus replied to Simon, "Don't be afraid! From now on you'll be fishing for people!" And as soon as they landed, they left everything and followed Jesus." (Luke 5:1–11)

Mark's and Matthew's accounts of this event are a bit hard for me to swallow. I would not drop everything and follow a virtual stranger simply because he or she told me to. I don't know many people who would do that. Luke's additional details make it more believable. I imagine Peter must have been impressed or touched by Jesus's teaching, which was why he called him "Master" and took his boat out again on Jesus's "say so." When their nets became filled to overflowing with fish, Peter "realized what had happened" and reacted with humility. Peter seems to have known at this point that Jesus was someone special and extraordinary. He must have realized that, because he walked away from his life in Capernaum to follow Jesus.

Even though Peter turned his whole life upside down to follow Jesus, I believe it is highly unlikely that Peter grasped who Jesus truly was when he first became his disciple. I believe it is much more likely that this understanding developed over time as he watched and listened to Jesus.

Watching and listening

Immediately after Peter began to follow him, "Jesus traveled throughout the region of Galilee, teaching in the synagogues and announcing the Good News about the Kingdom. And he healed every kind of disease and illness. News about him spread as far as Syria, and people soon began bringing to him all who were sick. And whatever their sickness or disease, or if they were demon possessed or epileptic or paralyzed—he healed them all" (Matthew 4:23–24).

The four Gospels are full of accounts of Jesus teaching and healing. We don't know for sure that Peter was with Jesus when all of these events occurred; however, we can be fairly certain that he was present for most, if not all, of these occurrences. Some of these events (a fraction of the miraculous events recorded that Jesus did during his three-year earthly ministry) are as follows:

- Changed water into wine at the wedding feast in Cana. (John 2:1–11)
- Healed a man with leprosy. (Mark 1:40–45; Matthew 8:1–4; Luke 5:12–16)
- Healed a paralyzed man. (Mark 2:1–12; Matthew 9:1–8; Luke 5:17–26)
- Healed a lame man. (John 5:1–15)

- Healed demon-possessed men.
  (Mark 1:21–26; Matthew 12:22–23)
- Raised a widow's son from the dead.
  (Luke 7:11–17)

We can assume that Peter was indeed present at an event involving his mother-in-law and witnessed the following happenings: "When Jesus arrived at Peter's house, Peter's mother-in-law was sick in bed with a high fever. But when Jesus touched her hand, the fever left her. Then she got up and prepared a meal for him. That evening many demon-possessed people were brought to Jesus. He cast out the evil spirits with a simple command, and he healed all the sick" (Matthew 8:14–16).

After hearing and seeing all that Jesus said and did during this time, Peter must have, at the very least, been entertaining the notion that Jesus was indeed the Son of God, the long-awaited Messiah.

I would now like to describe a series of events that, due to the way they are recorded in the four Gospels, seemingly occurred consecutively over the period of a day or two.

As evening came, Jesus said to his disciples, "Let's cross to the other side of the lake." So they took Jesus in the boat and started out, leaving the crowds behind (although other boats followed). But soon a fierce storm came up. High waves were breaking into the boat, and it began to fill with water.

Jesus was sleeping at the back of the boat with his head on a cushion. The disciples woke him up, shouting, "Teacher, don't you care that we're going to drown?"

When Jesus woke up, he rebuked the wind and said to the waves, "Silence! Be still!" Suddenly the wind stopped, and there was a great calm. Then he asked them, "Why are you afraid? Do you still have no faith?"

The disciples were absolutely terrified. "Who is this man?" they asked each other. "Even the wind and waves obey him!" (Mark 4:35–41)

Immediately after calming the storm, Jesus healed a demon-possessed man.

So they arrived at the other side of the lake, in the region of the Gerasenes. When Jesus climbed out of the boat, a man possessed by an evil spirit came out from a cemetery to meet him. This man lived among the burial caves and could no longer be restrained, even with a chain. Whenever he was put into chains and shackles—as he often was—he snapped the chains from his wrists and smashed the shackles. No one was strong enough to subdue him. Day and night he wandered among the burial caves and in the hills, howling and cutting himself with sharp stones.

When Jesus was still some distance away, the man saw him, ran to meet him, and bowed low before him. With a shriek, he screamed, "Why are you interfering with me, Jesus, Son of the Most High God? In the name of God, I beg you, don't torture me!" For Jesus had already said to the spirit, "Come out of the man, you evil spirit."

Then Jesus demanded, "What is your name?"

And he replied, "My name is Legion, because there are many of us inside this man." Then the evil spirits begged him again and again not to send them to some distant place.

There happened to be a large herd of pigs feeding on the hillside nearby. "Send us into those pigs," the spirits begged, "Let us enter them."

So Jesus gave them permission. The evil spirits came out of the man and entered the pigs, and the entire herd of about 2,000 pigs plunged down the steep hillside into the lake and drowned in the water.

The herdsmen fled to the nearby town and the surrounding countryside, spreading the news as they ran. People rushed out to see what had happened. A crowd soon gathered around Jesus, and they saw the man who had been possessed by the legion of demons. He was sitting there fully clothed and perfectly sane, and they were all afraid. (Mark 5:1–15)

Then, after healing the demon-possessed man, Jesus healed a woman with constant bleeding and raised a young girl from the dead.

Jesus got into the boat again and went back to the other side of the lake, where a large crowd gathered around him on the shore. Then a leader of the local synagogue, whose name was Jairus, arrived. When he saw Jesus, he fell at his feet, pleading fervently with him. "My little daughter is dying," he said. "Please come and lay your hands on her; heal her so she can live."

Jesus went with him, and all the people followed, crowding around him. A woman in the crowd had suffered for twelve years with constant bleeding. She had suffered a great deal from many doctors, and over the years she had spent everything she had to pay them, but she had gotten no better. In fact, she had gotten worse. She had heard about Jesus, so she came up behind him through the crowd and touched his robe. For she thought to herself, "If I can just touch his robe, I will be healed." Immediately the bleeding stopped, and she could feel in her body that she had been healed of her terrible condition.

Jesus realized at once that healing power had gone out from him, so he turned around in the crowd and asked, "Who touched my robe?"

His disciples said to him, "Look at this crowd pressing around you. How can you ask 'Who touched me?'"

But he kept on looking around to see who had done it. Then the frightened woman, trembling at the realization of what had happened to her, came and fell to her knees in front of him and told him what she had done. And he said to her, "Daughter, your faith has made you well. Go in peace. Your suffering is over."

While he was speaking to her, messengers arrived from the home of Jairus, the leader of the synagogue. They told him, "Your daughter is dead. There's no use troubling the Teacher now."

But Jesus overheard them and said to Jairus, "Don't be afraid. Just have faith."

Then Jesus stopped the crowd and wouldn't let anyone go with him except Peter, James, and John (the brother of James). When they came to the home of the synagogue leader, Jesus saw much commotion and weeping and wailing. He went inside and asked, "Why all this commotion and weeping? The child isn't dead; she's only asleep."

The crowd laughed at him. But he made them all leave, and he took the girl's father and mother and his three disciples into the room where the girl was lying. Holding her hand, he said to her, "*Talitha koum*," which means "Little girl, get up!" And the girl, who was twelve years old, immediately stood up and walked around! They were overwhelmed and totally amazed. (Mark 5:21–42)

After he left Jairus's home, "two blind men followed along behind him, shouting, 'Son of David, have mercy on us!' They went right into the house where he was staying, and Jesus asked them, 'Do you believe I can make you see?' 'Yes, Lord,' they told him, 'we do.' Then he touched their eyes and said, 'Because of your faith, it will happen.' Then their eyes were opened, and they could see!" (Matthew 9:27–30).

Jesus still wasn't finished for the day. After this "a demon-possessed man who couldn't speak was brought to Jesus. So Jesus cast out the demon, and then the man began to speak" (Matthew 9:32–33).

Peter must have been on sensory overload by this time, totally overwhelmed by what he had experienced. It is not certain that, by the end of this day, Peter truly believed that Jesus was the Son of God, the long-awaited Messiah. It is hard to imagine, though, that he wouldn't have believed by this point after all he had seen and heard. At some point Peter obviously did embrace the truth that Jesus truly was the Son of God, the long-awaited Messiah, because he stepped out of his comfort zone in a huge way.

Embracing the truth

Immediately after this, Jesus insisted that his disciples get back into the boat and cross to the other side of the lake, while he sent the people home. After sending them home, he went up into the hills by himself to pray. Night fell while he was there alone.

Meanwhile, the disciples were in trouble far away from land, for a strong wind had risen, and they were fighting heavy waves. About three o'clock in the morning Jesus came toward them, walking on the water. When the disciples saw him walking on the water, they were terrified. In their fear, they cried out, "It's a ghost!"

But Jesus spoke to them at once. "Don't be afraid," he said. "Take courage. I am here!"

Then Peter called to him, "Lord, if it's really you, tell me to come to you, walking on the water."

"Yes, come," Jesus said.

So Peter went over the side of the boat and walked on the water toward Jesus. But when he saw the strong wind and the waves, he was terrified and began to sink. "Save me, Lord!" he shouted.

Jesus immediately reached out and grabbed him. "You have so little faith," Jesus said. "Why did you doubt me?"

When they climbed back into the boat, the wind stopped. Then the disciples worshiped him. "You really are the Son of God!" they exclaimed. (Matthew 14:22–33)

After this, Peter's belief that Jesus was the Son of God seems to have become deeply rooted in him. He became bolder. He evidenced this boldness and certainty in the following incidents: "Many of his disciples turned away and deserted him. Then Jesus turned to the Twelve and asked, 'Are you also going to leave?' Simon Peter replied, 'Lord, to whom would we go? You have the words that give eternal life. We believe, and we know you are the Holy One of God'" (John 6:66–69).

"Jesus and his disciples left Galilee and went up to the villages near Caesarea Philippi. As they were walking along, he asked them, 'Who do people say I am?' 'Well,' they replied, 'some say John the Baptist, some say Elijah, and others say you are one of the other prophets.' Then he asked them, 'But who do you say I am?' Peter replied, 'You are the Messiah'" (Mark 8:27–29).

Jesus rewarded Peter's boldness and statements of certainty by allowing him to experience the following:

> Jesus took Peter and the two brothers, James and John, and led them up a high mountain to be alone. As the men watched, Jesus' appearance was transformed so that his face shone like the sun, and his clothes became as white as light. Suddenly, Moses and Elijah appeared and began talking with Jesus.
>
> Peter exclaimed, "Lord, it's wonderful for us to be here! If you want, I'll make three shelters as memorials—one for you, one for Moses, and one for Elijah."
>
> But even as he spoke, a bright cloud overshadowed them, and a voice from the cloud said, "This is my dearly loved Son, who brings me great joy. Listen to him." The disciples were terrified and fell face down on the ground.
>
> Then Jesus came over and touched them. "Get up," he said. "Don't be afraid." And when they looked up, Moses and Elijah were gone, and they saw only Jesus. (Matthew 17:1–8)

I imagine this must have completely cemented Peter's belief that Jesus really was the Son of God, the long-awaited Messiah. I'm also guessing that Jesus must have known

Peter would need the memory of this experience to carry him through the days, weeks, months, and years that were ahead of him.

Definition change

During one of the times Jesus appeared to the disciples after his crucifixion, Peter changed his definition of success.

> Later, Jesus appeared again to the disciples beside the Sea of Galilee. This is how it happened. Several of the disciples were there—Simon Peter, Thomas (nicknamed the Twin), Nathanael from Cana in Galilee, the sons of Zebedee, and two other disciples.
>
> Simon Peter said, "I'm going fishing."
>
> "We'll come, too," they all said. So they went out in the boat, but they caught nothing all night.
>
> At dawn Jesus was standing on the beach, but the disciples couldn't see who he was. He called out, "Fellows, have you caught any fish?"
>
> "No," they replied.
>
> Then he said, "Throw out your net on the right-hand side of the boat, and you'll get some!" So they did, and they couldn't haul in the net because there were so many fish in it.
>
> Then the disciple Jesus loved said to Peter, "It's the Lord!" When Simon Peter heard that it was the Lord, he put on his tunic (for he had stripped for work), jumped into the water, and headed to shore. The others stayed with the boat and pulled the loaded net to the shore,

for they were only about a hundred yards from shore. When they got there, they found breakfast waiting for them—fish cooking over a charcoal fire, and some bread.

"Bring some of the fish you've just caught," Jesus said. So Simon Peter went aboard and dragged the net to the shore. There were 153 large fish, and yet the net hadn't torn.

"Now come and have some breakfast!" Jesus said. None of the disciples dared to ask him, "Who are you?" They knew it was the Lord. Then Jesus served them the bread and the fish. This was the third time Jesus had appeared to his disciples since he had been raised from the dead." (John 21:1–14).

Bruce Wilkinson, in his book *Secrets of the Vine,* discussed the above incident. He wrote:

Apparently without hesitation, the men in their battered boats pull in their nets and fling them over the other side. Soon they haul up such a net-straining catch of fish that they know beyond doubt who that man in the mist is. "It is the Lord," John says to Peter. And you know what Peter does next. In your mind's eye you can see Peter look toward shore. You can see him drop his hold on the net, plant his foot on the bow of the boat, and take that beautiful, flying leap into the waters of grace . . . When Peter jumped, he forever left behind his little dreams of success. He left behind his doubts about God's plans for him and his stubborn insistence that things should turn out according to his expectations. He left behind any thought that his sins outweighed God's forgiveness. That impulsive leap marked the moment of Peter's breakthrough to a life of remarkable abundance ... God used him to be the new church's first leader, to preach to thousands, and to bring healing and the Holy Spirit.[108]

In that moment Peter changed his definition of success. He shifted forever from fishing for fish to fishing for people. Jesus then challenged Peter. I believe Jesus was testing Peter's commitment to follow him.

> After breakfast Jesus asked Simon Peter, "Simon son of John, do you love me more than these?"
>
> "Yes, Lord," Peter replied, "you know I love you."
>
> "Then feed my lambs," Jesus told him.
>
> Jesus repeated the question: "Simon son of John, do you love me?"
>
> "Yes, Lord," Peter said, "you know I love you."
>
> "Then take care of my sheep," Jesus said.
>
> A third time he asked him, "Simon son of John, do you love me?"
>
> Peter was hurt that Jesus asked the question a third time. He said, "Lord, you know everything. You know that I love you."
>
> Jesus said, "Then feed my sheep." (John 21:15–17)

Jesus then went on to tell Peter, "'I tell you the truth, when you were young, you were able to do as you liked; you dressed yourself and went wherever you wanted to go. But when you are old, you will stretch out your hands, and others will dress you and take you where you don't want to go'" (John 21:18). "The expression 'to stretch out your hands,' means absolutely nothing to us today, but to a person of Peter's time it was a clear reference to crucifixion."[109]

I believe it is a distinct possibility that Jesus asked Peter the same question (Do you love me?) three times and gave him the same command (in essence, Take care of my followers) three times because Jesus needed to drive home to Peter that it would be Peter's love for Jesus that would be the driving force, the motivator that would carry Peter to complete the work Jesus had assigned to him.

The last time Jesus appeared to the apostles he told them, "'I have been given all authority in heaven and on earth. Therefore, go and make disciples of all the nations, baptizing them in the name of the Father and the Son and the Holy Spirit. Teach these new disciples to obey all the commands I have given you. And be sure of this: I am with you always, even to the end of the age'" (Matthew 28:18–20).

"When the Lord Jesus had finished talking with them, he was taken up into heaven and sat down in the place of honor at God's right hand. And the disciples went everywhere and preached, and the Lord worked through them, confirming what they said by many miraculous signs" (Mark 16:19–20).

As Peter and the other apostles went about preaching, they were harassed and arrested by religious leaders, who repeatedly ordered them not to teach about Jesus. The apostles, however, did not let human beings stop them from doing the work they had been commissioned and anointed to do. "Peter and the apostles replied, 'We must obey God rather than any human authority'" (Acts 5:29). The religious leaders then stepped up their opposition against the apostles. This did not, however, deter the apostles one bit. They continued to teach and to heal in Jesus's name. "So God's message continued to spread. The number of believers greatly increased in Jerusalem, and many of the Jewish priests were converted, too" (Acts 6:7).

Peter was eventually arrested and imprisoned. The prison guards were not able to keep him in prison, though. God sent an angel to set him free (see Appendix 2). Following this incident,

> Peter seemed never to have returned to Jerusalem to stay . . . Peter spent many years traveling throughout the Near East. He visited the Christian communities which were springing up all over that area, preaching, teaching, and making sure that the new converts fell into no heresy . . . Peter also resided for a time in Antioch. A large city of about a million people, it was located in what is now the nation of Syria, about seventeen miles east of the Mediterranean coast.[110]

> Peter eventually went to Rome and lived there during his latter years . . . There were between thirty and forty thousand Jews living in Rome in the first century . . . Peter's popularity increased rapidly with many converts made in Rome.[111]

On the night of July 19, A.D. 64, fire broke out in a wooden shed at the foot of the Caelian and Palatine hills in Rome, and spread to the small shops nearby. Within hours, much of the city was engulfed by flames which burned out of control for nine days, destroying two thirds of Rome and killing hundreds. Nero ... blamed the Christians for the disaster. Had not Peter and Paul publicly proclaimed that the world would end in fire? Therefore, they must have been responsible. He denounced Christianity as a "deadly superstition," and accused Christians of being haters of the human race and perpetrators of such crimes as drinking the blood of babies in Holy Communion. Thus he marked the Church for extermination.[112]

Eventually, on a date no one is exactly sure of, Peter was crucified. According to William Steuart McBirnie in his book *The Search for the Twelve Apostles*, Peter spent nine months in a Roman prison prior to his death.

Maliciously condemned, Peter was cast into the horrible, fetid prison of the Mamertine. There, for nine months, in absolute darkness, he endured monstrous torture manacled to a post ... This dreaded place is known by two names. In classical history it is referred to as Gemonium or the Tullian Keep. In later secular history it is best known as the Mamertine ... The Mamertine is described as a deep cell cut out of solid rock at the foot of the capitol, consisting of two chambers, one over the other. The only entrance is through an aperture in the ceiling. The lower chamber was the death cell. Light never entered and it was never cleaned. The awful stench and filth generated a poison fatal to the inmates of the dungeon, the most awful ever known . . . How Peter managed to survive those nine long dreadful months is beyond human imagination. During his entire incarceration he was manacled in an upright position, chained to the column, unable to lay down to rest . . . History tells us the amazing fact that in spite of all the suffering Peter was subjected to, he converted his gaolers, Processus, Martinianus, and forty-seven others.[113]

I would hypothesize that Peter managed to complete the work assigned to him, as well as survive his imprisonment and convert his jailers, because he was a tough, strong, fearless fisherman who changed his definition of success and who was empowered by the Holy Spirit to weather fierce storms.

CHAPTER EIGHT

PAUL'S STORY

Paul (whose name at birth was Saul) was not only the second most influential leader of the early church but was perhaps its most influential missionary. He met Jesus in an unusual and powerful way. He then implemented a major course correction for his life and did what he was created to do.

Beginnings

Paul grew up in a Jewish family in the city of Tarsus in south-central Turkey, about 12 miles inland from the Mediterranean Sea. Tarsus, quite unlike the fishing village in which Peter grew up, "was a city of culture and politics, of philosophy and industry. Among those industries was a thriving textile business."[114] Tarsus, "like every ancient non-Jewish city, was full of shrines, full of strange worship, full of human lives misshapen by dehumanizing practices."[115] It "was full of talk, philosophical talk, speculation, logic, wise and not so wise advice about life, death, the gods, virtue, the way to an untroubled existence."[116] This talk (discussion, debate, argument, and so forth) not only took place in classrooms with teachers and serious-minded students;

it spilled out into the city, into taverns, shops, stalls in the marketplace, all kinds of businesses and industries. Therefore, "The Jewish world in which the young Saul grew up was itself firmly earthed in the soil of wider Greco-Roman culture"[117]

Saul's family was not merely Jewish, they belonged to the strictest sect of the Jews, the Pharisees. They believed and practiced the strictest of obedience to all the Jewish laws, customs, and ancestral traditions. They not only believed in this and practiced it themselves; they did their best to urge other Jews to do the same.

Saul was educated in Jerusalem under Gamaliel, one of the most honored rabbis of the time, "an expert in religious law and respected by all the people" (Acts 5:34). Gamaliel would be sure to have trained young Saul thoroughly in Jewish law and customs. The narrative that the young Saul of Tarsus learned and embraced was this:

> The One God, so the prophets had said, abandoned his house in Jerusalem because of the people's idolatry and sin. But successive prophets . . . had promised that he would return one day . . . though the Temple still held powerful memories of divine presence . . . there was a strong sense that the promise of ultimate divine return had not yet been fulfilled . . . The God of Israel had said he would return, but had not done so yet . . . Saul of Tarsus was brought up to believe that it would happen, perhaps very soon. Israel's God would indeed return in glory to establish his kingdom in

visible global power. He was also taught that there were things Jews could be doing in the meantime to keep this promise and hope on track. Keep the Torah with rigorous attention to detail and to defend the Torah, and the Temple itself, against possible attacks and threats. Failure on these points would hold back the promise, would get in the way of the fulfillment of the great story.[118]

We know from the letters Paul wrote decades later to the churches he planted that he was a tentmaker. This is how he supported himself financially as he traveled from city to city on his missionary journeys. It would seem logical, then, that Saul's family, living in a city with a thriving textile business, were tentmakers and that Saul had been taught this trade as a young man.

"It seems improbable that a Jewish tentmaker in a city like Tarsus would be selling only to other Jews. We can safely assume, then, that Saul grew up in a cheerfully strict observant Jewish home, on the one hand, and in a polyglot, multicultural, multiethnic working environment on the other."[119] It also seems probable that the talks, discussions, debates, and so forth referenced above may very well have taken place in his family's tentmaking shop.

"Everything we know about him encourages us to think of the young Saul of Tarsus as an unusually gifted child. He read biblical Hebrew fluently. He spoke the Aramaic of the Middle East . . . in addition to the ubiquitous Greek, which he spoke and wrote at great speed. He probably had at least some Latin . . . He gives every impression of having swallowed the Bible whole."[120] It therefore seems highly likely that young Saul could and did hold his own while discussing and debating these issues with adults.

When Saul first learned of Jesus and his followers, he did not embrace the belief that Jesus was the promised Messiah. Quite the contrary, he was an avid and zealous persecutor of the first Christians.

Saul's fuel

The Jewish narrative that young Saul learned and wholeheartedly embraced fueled his persecution of the early Christ followers. "From the point of view of Saul of Tarsus, the first followers of Jesus of Nazareth were a prime example of the deviant behavior that had to be eradicated if Israel's God was to be honored. Saul of Tarsus was therefore 'zealous' in persecuting these people."[121] In Sam Hunter's words, "He was a real stickler for the law, extraordinarily bright and intellectual, with a tenacious personality."[122]

The first time Saul's name appears in the Bible is when Stephen was being stoned. Stephen was one of seven men appointed by the twelve apostles to minister to new believers in Jerusalem. He was "a man full of God's grace and power, performed amazing miracles and signs among the people" (Acts 6:8). One day some men from one of the synagogues debated with him. "None of them could stand against the wisdom and the Spirit with which Stephen spoke" (Acts 6:10). So, some of them lied about Stephen to the Jewish elders and teachers of religious law. This resulted in Stephen being arrested and brought before the Jewish high council. When questioned about the statements made about him, Stephen launched into a lengthy discourse about the history of their ancestors. He ended with,

> You stubborn people! You are heathen at heart and deaf to the truth. Must you forever resist the Holy Spirit? That's what your ancestors did, and so do you! Name one prophet your ancestors didn't persecute! They even killed the ones who predicted the coming of the Righteous One—the Messiah whom you betrayed and murdered. You deliberately disobeyed God's law, even though you received it from the hands of angels. (Acts 7:51–53)
>
> The Jewish leaders were infuriated by Stephen's accusation, and they shook their fists at him in rage . . . They rushed at him and dragged him out of the city and began to stone him. His accusers took off their coats and laid them at the feet of a young man named Saul . . . Saul was one of the witnesses, and he agreed completely with the killing of Stephen. (Acts 7:54, 57–58; 8:1)

Following Stephen's murder, the persecution of Jesus's followers in Jerusalem went into high gear. "Saul was going everywhere to destroy the church. He went from house to house, dragging out both men and women to throw them into prison" (Acts 8:3). He then set out for Damascus to arrest any followers of Jesus he could find in that city. "He wanted to bring them—both men and women—back to Jerusalem in chains" (Acts 9:2). Jesus grabbed hold of him in transit and changed his plan. (See Appendix 3.)

Following this experience, Saul abandoned his own agenda and embraced God's purpose for his life. He spent the rest of his days on earth telling anyone and everyone he could that Jesus Christ was the promised Messiah. He changed his definition of success from eradicating the church of Jesus Christ to planting and growing congregations of Jesus followers anywhere and everywhere he could.

"Then Barnabas went on to Tarsus to look for Saul. When he found him, he brought him back to Antioch. Both of them stayed there with the church for a full year, teaching large crowds of people. (It was at Antioch that the believers were first called Christians)" (Acts 11:25–26). "The believers in Antioch decided to send relief to the brothers and sisters in Judea, everyone giving as much as they could. This they did, entrusting their gifts to Barnabas and Saul to take to the elders of the church in Jerusalem" (Acts 11:29–30).

"When Barnabas and Saul had finished their mission to Jerusalem, they returned, taking John Mark with them" (Acts 12:25). One day as the leaders of the church in Antioch "were worshiping the Lord and fasting, the Holy Spirit said, 'Dedicate Barnabas and Saul for the special work to which I have called them.' So after more fasting and prayer, the men laid their hands on them and sent them on their way" (Acts 13:2–3).

Fulfilling his purpose

Paul then set out on the first of three missionary journeys. At Antioch Of Pisidia, a district in what is now Turkey, Paul and Barnabas were invited to preach in their synagogue.

Almost the entire city turned out to hear them preach the word of the Lord. But when some of the Jews saw the crowds, they were jealous; so they slandered Paul and argued against whatever he said.

Then Paul and Barnabas spoke out boldly and declared, "It was necessary that we first preach the word of God to you Jews. But since you have rejected it and judged yourselves unworthy of eternal life, we will offer it to the Gentiles. For the Lord gave us this command when he said,

'I have made you a light to the Gentiles, to bring salvation to the farthest corners of the earth.'" (Acts 13:44–47)

What happened next soon became the predictable, habitual response to their ministry. "Then the Jews stirred up the influential religious women and the leaders of the city, and they incited a mob against Paul and Barnabas and ran them out of town. So they shook the dust from their feet as a sign of rejection and went to the town of Iconium" (Acts 13:50–51).

The same thing happened in Iconium. Paul and Barnabas went to the Jewish synagogue and preached with such power that a great number of both Jews and Greeks became believers. Some of the Jews, however, spurned God's message and poisoned the minds of the Gentiles against Paul and Barnabas. But the apostles stayed there a long time, preaching boldly about the grace of the Lord. And the Lord proved their message was true by giving them power to do miraculous signs and wonders. But the people of the town were divided in their opinion about them. Some sided with the Jews, and some with the apostles.

Then a mob of Gentiles and Jews, along with their leaders, decided to attack and stone them. When the apostles learned of it, they fled to the region of Lycaonia—to the towns of Lystra and Derbe and the surrounding area. And there they preached the Good News. (Acts 14:1–7)

After preaching the Good News in Derbe and making many disciples, Paul and Barnabas returned to Lystra, Iconium, and Antioch of Pisidia, where they strengthened the believers. They encouraged them to continue in the faith, reminding them that we must suffer many hardships to enter the Kingdom of God. Paul and Barnabas also appointed elders in every church. With prayer and fasting, they turned the elders over to the care of the Lord, in whom they had put their trust. (Acts 14:21–23)

Finally, they returned by ship to Antioch of Syria, where their journey had begun. The believers there had entrusted them to the grace of God to do the work they had now completed. Upon arriving in Antioch, they called the church together and reported everything God had done through them and how he had opened the door of faith to the Gentiles, too. (Acts 14:26–27)

After spending an extended period of time in Antioch, Paul decided to depart on a second missionary journey. This time he chose Silas to be his traveling companion. As he left Antioch "the believers entrusted him to the Lord's gracious care. Then he traveled throughout Syria and Cilicia, strengthening the churches there" (Acts 15:40–41).

Early in this journey Paul and Silas met a young disciple named Timothy, who then accompanied them for the remainder of the journey.

While in Philippi, a Roman colony in Macedonia, Paul and Silas were arrested. Some of the citizens of the city

> grabbed Paul and Silas and dragged them before the authorities at the marketplace. "The whole city is in an uproar because of these Jews!" they shouted to the city officials. "They are teaching customs that are illegal for us Romans to practice."
>
> A mob quickly formed against Paul and Silas, and the city officials ordered them stripped and beaten with wooden rods. They were severely beaten, and then they were thrown into prison. The jailer was ordered to make sure they didn't escape. So the jailer put them into the inner dungeon and clamped their feet in the stocks. (Acts 16:19–24)

After only a few days the city officials released Paul and Silas from prison, and they continued on their journey. When they reached Thessalonica, Paul went to the synagogue service, and for three Sabbaths in a row he used the Scriptures to reason with the people. He explained the prophecies and proved that the Messiah must suffer and rise from the dead. He said, "This Jesus I'm telling you about is the Messiah." Some of the Jews who listened were persuaded and joined Paul and Silas, along with many God-fearing Greek men and quite a few prominent women.

But some of the Jews were jealous, so they gathered some troublemakers from the marketplace to form a mob and start a riot. (Acts 17:2–5)

That very night the believers sent Paul and Silas to Berea. When they arrived there, they went to the Jewish synagogue. And the people of Berea were more open-minded than those in Thessalonica, and they listened eagerly to Paul's message. They searched the Scriptures day after day to see if Paul and Silas were teaching the truth. As a result, many Jews believed, as did many of the prominent Greek women and men. (Acts 17:10–12)

From Berea Paul went to Athens, where he debated with some of the Epicurean and Stoic philosophers. Due to God having prepared him from birth, Paul was uniquely suited to do this. God had given him an extraordinary intellect, which he used to gain a thorough knowledge of both Jewish and Greek thought and beliefs. God had also placed him in an environment where he could be trained to discuss and debate. Due to this, it is highly likely that Paul held his own with the philosophers.

Paul then went to Corinth, where he stayed for approximately two years. He then visited Ephesus, as well as other cities, before returning to Antioch. After spending some time in Antioch, he left for his third and final missionary journey. Timothy and several other men accompanied him. One of their first destinations was Ephesus.

> Then Paul went to the synagogue and preached boldly for the next three months, arguing persuasively about the Kingdom of God. But some became stubborn, rejecting his message and publicly speaking against the Way. So Paul left the synagogue and took the believers with him. Then he held daily discussions at the lecture hall of Tyrannus. This went on for the next two years, so that people throughout the province of Asia—both Jews and Greeks—heard the word of the Lord. (Acts 19:8–10)

When Paul left Ephesus, he visited several other cities before ending up not far from Ephesus. Before he sailed for Jerusalem he met with the Ephesian elders. During that meeting he told them, "My life is worth nothing to me unless I use it for finishing the work assigned me by the Lord Jesus—the work of telling others the Good News about the wonderful grace of God" (Acts 20:24).

When Paul arrived in Jerusalem he was arrested by some Jewish leaders and charged with "undermining the Torah and defiling the Temple. These were, in other words, charges of radical disloyalty to the Jewish world and its ancestral heritage."[123] He was then handed over to the Roman government. While he was in prison in Jerusalem, "the Lord appeared to Paul and said, 'Be encouraged, Paul. Just as you have been a witness to me here in Jerusalem, you must preach the Good News in Rome as well'" (Acts 23:11).

When the commander of the prison in Jerusalem learned of a plot to kill Paul, he had him removed from the prison under armed escort and taken to Caesarea, where he was imprisoned for approximately two years. When he stood before Festus, the Roman governor in Caesarea,

> Paul denied the charges. "I am not guilty of any crime against the Jewish laws or the Temple or the Roman government," he said.
>
> Then Festus, wanting to please the Jews, asked him, "Are you willing to go to Jerusalem and stand trial before me there?"
>
> But Paul replied, "No! This is the official Roman court, so I ought to be tried right here. You know very well I am not guilty of harming the Jews. If I have done something worthy of death, I don't refuse to die. But if I am innocent, no one has a right to turn me over to these men to kill me. I appeal to Caesar!"
>
> Festus conferred with his advisors and then replied, "Very well! You have appealed to Caesar, and to Caesar you will go!" (Acts 25:8–12)

So, to Rome he was sent to stand trial before Caesar. When Paul arrived in Rome, he was not put in prison. Rather, he was placed in a private residence, guarded by a soldier to await his trial. "So now he stuck to his principles and his habits and—assuming he was under house arrest and could not attend a synagogue himself—invited the leaders of the Jewish community to call on him."[124]

"For the next two years, Paul lived in Rome at his own expense. He welcomed all who visited him, boldly proclaiming the Kingdom of God and teaching about the Lord Jesus Christ. And no one tried to stop him" (Acts 28:30–31).

Paul's letters

While traveling on his missionary journeys and under house arrest in Rome, Paul wrote letters to churches he had planted and to individuals serving as pastors and leaders in these churches. The letters were meant to offer instruction, encouragement, and correction to both congregations and individuals. They still serve as such today.

Paul wrote his letter to the church in Rome while in Corinth. He wrote it several years before he actually arrived in Rome as a way of introducing himself to the congregation in anticipation of a future visit to them. He wrote two letters to the church in Corinth, one while he was in Ephesus and one while in Macedonia. He wrote two letters to the church in Thessalonica. Both of these letters were written during his second missionary journey. His letter to the church in Ephesus and his letter to the church in Colosse were written from Rome.

In his letter to the church in Galatia, written sometime during the third missionary journey, Paul told them about his conversion and subsequent actions:

> Dear brothers and sisters, I want you to understand that the gospel message I preach is not based on mere human reasoning. I received my message from no human source, and no one taught me. Instead I received it by direct revelation from Jesus Christ.
>
> You know what I was like when I followed the Jewish religion—how I violently persecuted God's church. I did my best to destroy it. I was far ahead of my fellow Jews in my zeal for the traditions of my ancestors.
>
> But even before I was born, God chose me and called me by his marvelous grace. Then it pleased him to reveal his Son to me so that I would proclaim the Good News about Jesus to the Gentiles.
>
> When this happened, I did not rush out to consult with any human being. Nor did I go up to Jerusalem to consult with those who were apostles before I was. Instead, I went away into Arabia, and later I returned to the city of Damascus.
>
> Then three years later I went to Jerusalem to get to know Peter, and I stayed with him for fifteen days. The only other apostle I met at that time was James, the Lord's brother. I declare

before God that what I am writing to you is not a lie.

After that visit I went north into the provinces of Syria and Cilicia. And still the churches in Christ that are in Judea didn't know me personally. All they knew was that people were saying, "The one who used to persecute us is now preaching the very faith he tried to destroy!" And they praised God because of me. (Galatians 1:11–24)

In his letter to the church in Philippi, written in Rome, he shared how he managed to endure trials and hardships and keep going:

I have learned how to be content with whatever I have. I know how to live on almost nothing or with everything. I have learned the secret of living in every situation, whether it is with a full stomach or empty, with plenty or little. For I can do everything through Christ, who gives me strength. (Philippians 4:11–13)

He wrote two letters to Timothy while in Rome. In the second letter he stated, "As for me, my life has already been poured out as an offering to God. The time of my death is near. I have fought the good fight, I have finished the race, and I have remained faithful" (2 Timothy 4:6–7).

Paul's story ends here. No one knows how, when, or where Paul died. What we do know is that, by the end of his life, he was instrumental in bringing the good news of Jesus Christ to much of the Mediterranean world. Hence, he was one of the most, if not *the* most, influential missionary of the early church.

CHAPTER NINE

21ST-CENTURY DISCIPLES

Jesus is still calling people to be his disciples. That did not end when he stopped walking the earth in the flesh. Below are stories of two individuals who said yes to his call, carrying on his work in the world today. I know one of these individuals personally. The other I read about in J. Lee Grady's book *10 Lies the Church Tells Women*.

Becky's story

Becky grew up as the fourth of five children on a dairy farm near Titusville, Pennsylvania, the birthplace of the American Oil Industry. In addition to 80 Holstein cows, 1,000 chickens, pigs, geese, ducks, a ram, and a horse, they also had 15 working oil wells on their property. The oil that they pumped was then sold to Quaker State. To help make ends meet, her father also worked in the local steel mill.

Becky began doing household chores at an early age. She switched to farm chores though as soon as she was old enough as she never liked doing housework. Her favorite chore was helping her father. She worked alongside him wherever he was working. This included repairing and maintaining farm equipment; milking cows; gathering, washing, weighing, and casing eggs; planting and harvesting hay, oats, wheat, buckwheat, and corn; and pumping or pulling the oil wells.

The family attended a local Free Methodist Church. They went to services on Sunday mornings and evenings, as well Wednesday evening prayer meetings. They also attended weeklong revival meetings whenever they were held. In addition, Becky attended Sunday school and youth group.

During the Sunday services there was a group of spinsters and widows who sat together in the pews at the back of the church. Before each service they would share their weekly activities and gossip with each other.

Becky described her childhood church experience in the following words:

> The sermons were fire and brimstone teachings. I grew up learning a worldly fear of God. I certainly didn't want to go to hell, so I asked for God's forgiveness and accepted him into my heart at the age of thirteen during a revival meeting. I don't really remember learning much about Jesus. I certainly knew God, and I knew that the Holy Spirit was within us. I guess I knew that Jesus was our Savior, but I didn't understand at that time that he was my redeemer, or what it meant to have a personal relationship with him.

When Becky was sixteen and a junior in high school, the house on the neighboring farm, owned by her aunt and uncle, caught fire a few days after Christmas. She could see the smoke and flames from her house and ran the quarter mile to her cousins' house. Everyone got out alive, and "we stood by the road and just watched it burn until morning when the entire house was reduced to smoldering ash."

Her aunt and uncle rented a house in a nearby town to live in while they built a new home. Becky would occasionally ride the school bus home with her cousin Kathy to spend the weekend with them. One Friday when she was on the way to her cousin's house, she was introduced to a boy on the bus. He started coming to her cousin's house to visit when she was there. They eventually started dating. Toward the end of summer, Becky started feeling sick and having lighter periods. In early November her mother scheduled a doctor's appointment for her. With her mother in the room, the doctor asked if there was a chance she could be pregnant. Her answer was yes.

> My mind was catapulted into a dizzying state as I started worrying about what I would do. I contemplated suicide, but my thinking at that time was that I didn't want to go to hell, which was what we had been taught happened if you committed suicide, nor did I want to kill my baby. Being young and naive, I contemplated running away, but I couldn't formulate a plan to earn an income or find a place to live. Abortion or adoption was never something that I considered.

I loved my boyfriend and wanted to keep our baby. At some point our parents met and decided that we should get married.

She and her boyfriend discussed getting married and decided that "We were best friends first before we started dating. We both felt that even if I hadn't gotten pregnant, we would eventually get married because we wanted to spend our lives together." They were married on December 20, 1975, in the church she attended when staying with her cousin Kathy. It was a small wedding in the church parsonage with both sets of parents. Kathy was her witness, and her boyfriend's best friend was his witness. "It was a beautiful winter day, the snow falling gently, and we were married. We had a small reception with family at my parents' house." She added, "After nearly 45 years, we are still married, are still best friends and love each other deeply."

Her sister and brother-in-law lived on a parcel of the family farm and had a finished basement that Becky and her husband rented. It was their first home, and they spent their honeymoon there. The morning after the wedding Becky woke up bleeding. They walked the eighth of a mile to her parents' house, as they had no car or phone. Her parents drove them to the hospital, where Becky was told by the doctor that they couldn't detect a heartbeat and she was going to lose the baby. She was 5½ months pregnant.

They whisked me off to a room and all I can remember is lying there vomiting and hemorrhaging and this kindly older nurse bringing a cool cloth for my forehead. She kept saying "you poor child". She stayed by my side as much as she could all day long. After a while, she called in the doctor because I must have been delivering the baby. I saw him with the baby in his hand and heard them say it was a boy. The baby was placed in a stainless-steel bowl and, as he exited the room, the doctor placed the contents of the bowl, my baby, in a waste can in the corner of the room. Around midnight I was taken into surgery because I had not delivered the placenta and was still hemorrhaging. After receiving four pints of blood and spending four days in the hospital, I was discharged on Christmas Eve and we went to stay with my husband's parents for a few weeks so my mother-in-law could help take care of me while I recovered.

Once she recovered, they returned to their home in her sister's basement and went back to school. The guidance counselor arranged for both of them to get jobs through the Job Training Partnership Act (JTPA), a federal assistance program that prepared youth and unskilled adults for entry into the labor force and provided *job training* to economically disadvantaged and other individuals facing serious barriers to employment. Becky and her husband rode the bus to school in the morning, attended classes for half a day, walked to their jobs, walked back to school, and rode the bus home. Becky worked as a supply clerk at the local hospital, and her husband was a groundskeeper at the Drake Well Museum, where oil was discovered. Her parents took them into town on Friday nights to get groceries. They did this until the end of their Senior year, when they both graduated with their class.

A fallout from Becky's out-of-wedlock teenage pregnancy was that she stopped going to church.

> I felt that I had sinned and angered God. I dropped out of church because I felt the shame was too great to face anyone. I believed that I had disappointed my parents, disobeyed God, embarrassed the pastor, and was certain the ladies in the back pew would all be gossiping about me. I suppose I never gave anyone in church the chance to find out how they would really treat me.

After graduation, Becky initially worked as a secretary for the local Chamber of Commerce through JTPA. She was then hired as a secretary for an accounting firm. One of the owners of the firm was a professor at the local campus of the University of Pittsburgh. She became a non-traditional student there, with the goal of earning an accounting degree. She worked full-time during the day and attended classes in the evening. In addition, she gave birth to a daughter in 1978. Her husband worked as a delivery person for an office supply company, a janitor at a retail store, and then was hired by a machine shop and trained as a machinist, specifically a CNC operator.

When she became pregnant with their second child, a son, in 1979, she quit working and attending classes to be a stay-at-home mother. She went back to work part-time two years later as a typesetter and an advertising and page layout artist for the local newspaper. She and her husband worked opposite shifts so they could share the childcare responsibilities. She went back to work full-time in 1983 as an accountant for a local lumber company and started attending evening classes again. She was eventually promoted to the position of Total Quality Manager for her division. About a year later, she was trained by a consulting firm the company hired to do Activity Value Analysis, a method of streamlining and improving efficiency. In the end, the company decided they weren't ready to implement the quality program at her facility, resulting in her position being eliminated in 1990. Jesus used this experience to speak to her heart.

> I had become a workaholic. In addition to fulfilling the roles of inventory control and production planner, I was facilitating quality circles with three shifts of employees, and still taking night classes. My "success" in my career defined my identity. When my position was terminated, I felt like I lost who I was. Even though my husband and family showed me unconditional love, there was a huge void in my life.
>
> Soon after my termination I received a phone call from one of the executives of the division asking what happened. She told me she was shocked, as a week earlier they were discussing my potential as general manager or controller. The division president had stated that there was no way in hell that he would have a female running one of his divisions. I had hit

the glass-ceiling. I decided to take time off work and school to heal. I took ceramics classes with a friend. The studio owner was an art major, and she showed us the beauty of expressing ourselves through painting and creating artistic pieces. This heightened my awareness of my surroundings, and I felt God calling to me through the beauty of his creation.

At that time the unemployment rate in Northwestern Pennsylvania was 13.8 percent. Though her husband was still working full-time as a machinist, the only jobs available for her were minimum wage jobs, which she was not willing to take. Her in-laws had moved to South Central Pennsylvania, and the job market was good there, so they relocated to Lancaster in 1991.

Her husband quickly found work as a machinist. Soon after that she secured a position as a Senior Accountant for a manufacturer. The company was sold in 2005 and again in 2010. She stayed with the company through both acquisitions, eventually moving into the position of Division Controller.

Soon after the move to Lancaster, Becky felt the need to connect with God and a church community. She started attending a local United Methodist church. One Sunday during a healing service, she felt called to the altar and recommitted her life to Christ. She followed this with participation in Disciple Bible Study, a 34-week class that studies the Bible from beginning to end. At the conclusion of this class, she joined the church and was baptized.

In 1994 Becky took on an additional part-time evening job as an accountant for a local start-up publishing company. As the business grew, she moved into the full-time position of business manager. The company quickly grew from three to twenty-one employees. As this role presented many new challenges for her, she searched for a support group that could help her become a better manager. She initially looked into a local Women's Club; however, since she was growing in her faith, she wanted to learn to lead through a spiritual lens.

She ended up joining the church's small group ministry, where she started a small group for working women (where we met). Many of the group leaders were in management positions in business. They proved to be the resource she was looking for to help her lead through a spiritual lens.

Side note: I was initially in Becky's group for working women. I then left that group and started a group for converts from Catholicism. When the invitation went out to all small group leaders to accompany the senior pastor to Saddleback Church in California to learn about Celebrate Recovery, Becky and I both decided to go.

When we got back to Pennsylvania, I knew beyond the shadow of a doubt that God wanted me to serve in the Celebrate Recovery ministry. Becky, however, wasn't sure. As she worked the 12 Steps, the shame and guilt she still carried inside her from her teenage pregnancy were healed. As she prayed for the Holy Spirit's guidance regarding where she was to serve, she came to realize that the purpose of her involvement in Celebrate Recovery was her own healing. It was not to be her ministry.

In the meantime, the small group she was leading had changed course from a working women's support group to a Bible study group. As the focus of the church's teaching at that time was the Prayer of Jabez ("'Oh, that you would bless me and expand my territory! Please be with me in all that I do, and keep me from all trouble and pain!'" [1 Chronicles 4:10]), the group started praying this prayer and asking God to show them where to serve. Becky asked her heavenly Father to show her where he was working so she could work alongside him, as she had with her earthly father. At one of the group meetings, discussion centered on the challenges the women were facing to clothe their children for the upcoming school year. God showed them that they weren't the only ones facing this challenge. They came to realize that this was a need in their community that they could do something about. They prayed about it and decided to host a clothing giveaway prior to the next school year. They got permission from church leadership to use the church social hall for one day the following August for the giveaway. As they started to collect clothing, donations poured in. One of the group members offered to store the clothing in her basement. By August, her basement, her living room, and every spare inch of her home were filled with clothing to give away.

During the first giveaway, the group members experienced the joy of giving through the smiles on the children's faces and the thanks extended to them from the parents for the clothing they received. The group members looked across the room at each other, and each one nodded yes! They all knew that this was their calling and that they had to do it again.

Becky and her husband rented a local garage to store the donations for the next giveaway. They added school supplies and a children's craft area to the next giveaway to keep the children occupied while their parents "shopped."

The amount of work involved to pull off the clothing giveaway was immense, and Becky realized that changes needed to be made in order to keep the ministry viable. The first change they made was to move the collection and storage of the clothing to the church. In response to a petition from the group, the church gave them storage space to do this. Since the school supplies were a hit, they also added a backpack giveaway. Each backpack was filled with grade appropriate school supplies for any child who needed them. The next change was to raise funds to support the ministry. With this came the need for accountability, so group members selected a treasurer and started attending workshops for non-profit groups at Leadership Lancaster to explore various systems of accountability.

Throughout this process God was showing Becky that she would burn out if she handled too much of the ministry herself. He was protecting her from her tendency toward workaholism. The solution to this was to create a leadership team to share the workload for the ministry. Six teams were created. Each team consisted of a leader and co-leader, and each was responsible for one area of the ministry, i.e., giveaway event coordination; media advertising; backpack and school supply collection and assembly; fundraising; children's corner ministry; and volunteer coordinators. "We recognized the 'twelve' disciples that God had provided for his ministry. It was clear from the beginning that this was not our ministry but God's ministry. It would be fruitful and grow as long as we stayed faithful in working alongside where God was working. God is so good!"

After the second giveaway event the group realized that this need for clothing existed throughout the year. Becky and another group member felt moved to establish a clothing bank at the church, which would operate year-round. They began to write a ministry action plan (similar to a business plan). As they did this, they visited several clothing banks at other churches to gain an understanding of exactly what was involved in operating such a ministry. At the end of one such visit,

> we joined hands with their members in a circle of prayer. As one of the women spoke to God, his spiritual presence was felt. As she prayed for God's anointing, I felt a hand pressed against my forehead, as if I was being anointed with oil. But this was impossible! All of our hands were joined in the circle. My fellow group member experienced the same thing! God had truly anointed us for this ministry.

They finished the action plan for the clothing bank, and the church council approved it. The stated goal of the ministry was to provide clothing for any person of any age who was in need. They were given the space they had requested and started to put the pieces in place to establish the clothing bank. It was launched with a grand opening celebration, including a consecration service by the senior pastor. Many groups and individuals from both the church and the community served in the ministry by sorting and hanging clothes and restocking the clothing store. One individual volunteered to be a personal shopper for families who didn't have the means to come to the clothing bank. This individual "shopped" for these families and delivered the items to their homes.

God impressed upon Becky that a legacy was needed for his work to continue. To that end, mission and vision statements were developed, and a board of directors was established. The board of directors consisted of a president, vice-president, secretary, treasurer, and three trustees to oversee the clothing bank, clothing giveaway, and other ministries that popped up occasionally to run in conjunction with the clothing ministry. Some of these ministries were a children's reading corner in the clothing bank established by one of the church's small groups, a sack lunch giveaway facilitated by a Sunday school class, and a soup can giveaway started by another small group.

As of this writing, the annual clothing giveaway has taken place for 18 consecutive years, and the clothing bank has been operating for 16 years. God has touched many lives through this ministry. A small sampling of the lives he has touched includes women who fled abusive situations and flew across the country with only the clothes on their back, women who found themselves and their children homeless and couldn't get help from social service agencies because they didn't have a permanent address, refugees from other countries who were resettling their families in the community, an elderly couple who shared that the two cans of soup they received would be their only hot meal for a week, and a clothing bank team member who experienced a deepening of her faith and trust in God.

Since the birth of the clothing giveaway, God has faithfully provided for his ministry.

> Each year we asked God to show us what our goals should be and provide us with the resources to meet that goal. We were mostly "Type A" personalities, and sometimes we would find ourselves relying on ourselves to meet the goals instead of relying on God. One year we were falling short of our monetary goal after exhausting our fundraising efforts. We prayed about this and were assured that God would provide whatever we were supposed to have. Our goal was to have 950 back packs filled with school supplies. Our budget was just under $12,000. Two weeks before we were to purchase the school supplies and pack the back packs, we were $4,000 short. Then, a team member was asked by a parishioner what we needed. The team member confided how much money we were short. The parishioner wrote a check for the deficit on the spot. Our hearts were touched, and our faith and trust in the Lord grew immensely. He will never forsake us.

Becky is no longer involved with the clothing ministry. She has moved on to shepherding a group of women who are mature in their faith and want to stay connected and support each other.

Jackie's story:

Jackie Rodriguez was a Florida housewife and mother of one small child when she began to accept invitations to preach in churches in her city. Her husband, Nuno, a pastor in Orlando, was baffled by his wife's decision to step out and assume such a high-profile role. But Jackie never once asked for a speaking engagement. Churches called her and begged her to minister. "I didn't ask to do this," she told Nuno once when he questioned her motives. "I have not once picked up the telephone and called anyone to ask them to schedule me. God is opening these doors." It was not an easy road for Jackie. In Hispanic culture, where machismo is a dominant force, women are expected to function in a purely domestic role. And Jackie soon found that machismo is also a powerful influence in Hispanic churches. When pastors heard her speak, they were shocked. She spoke with authority, but they could not reconcile her obvious anointing with the cultural traditions that held a vise grip on their minds. To them, Jackie was violating an unwritten law of Spanish culture. "Who do you think you are?" pastors would ask her. "You are coming across too strong. You are a woman!" they would scream. Some of the Hispanic women also opposed her, but Jackie pressed through the resistance and ultimately gained respect . . . In 1999, she and her husband became associate pastors at The Church of the People, a twelve-hundred-member Hispanic Charismatic congregation, in Mission, Texas, on the far eastern border of Mexico. Jackie began preaching sermons and airing a Spanish-language broadcast, Waves of Revival, that reaches thousands in the Mexican cities of Reynosa and Matamoros. She also began broadcasting to the entire region a television program featuring her relevant preaching. And people started responding to her message.

There are some leaders in the church today who would say that Jackie Rodriguez's ministry is illegitimate. If they could, they would yank her off the podiums and platforms where she stands and pull her TV and radio programs off the airwaves because they believe her gender disqualifies her from carrying the message of the gospel.[125]

As Isaiah told the people of Israel, God is sovereign, he knows what he is doing, and he chooses whomever he wants to do whatever he wants. The same holds true today.

CHAPTER TEN

ESSENTIAL ELEMENTS

All the individuals described in the previous chapters, both those pursuing their own definitions of success and those fulfilling a God-given purpose, share a specific set of personality characteristics and behaviors. These characteristics and behaviors include:

- Vision
- Passion
- Internal motivation
- Focus
- Teachability
- Risk taking
- Perseverance
- Willingness to do whatever it takes

Let's take these one at a time.

1. Vision

Vision is a picture of the future that only you can see.

As described in chapter two, Howard Schultz experienced a vision for the future of Starbucks while standing in an espresso bar in Milan. "As I watched, I had a revelation: Starbucks had missed the point—completely missed it. *This is so powerful!* I thought. *This is the link* ... The Italians understood the personal relationship that people could have to coffee, it's social aspect. I couldn't believe that Starbucks was in the coffee business, yet was overlooking so central an element of it. It was like an epiphany. It was so immediate and physical that I was shaking."

As described in chapter three, Bruce Springsteen developed a vision for his life one building block at a time while he was a child. The first building block was put in place when he was seven years old and watched Elvis Presley on the *Ed Sullivan Show*. The second building block was added when he held a concert for some neighborhood children in his backyard. The third building block was hearing the Beatles on the radio. The final building block was his realization that he didn't want to meet the Beatles; he wanted to BE the Beatles.

As described in chapter eight, the apostle Paul spent his post-conversion life planting churches throughout the known world on his missionary journeys and then nurturing these churches on subsequent visits and through his letters. It is clear in his various writings that Paul envisioned church bodies, or congregations, that preached and lived the values and lifestyle that Jesus modeled and taught. Paul envisioned churches that viewed and treated all persons as equal. In his letter to the church in Galatia, Paul stated, "There is no longer Jew or Gentile, slave or free, male and female. For you are all one in Christ Jesus" (Galatians 3:28).

As for myself, a vision for my life was birthed during a psychology course I took during my senior year in high school. As a result of that course, I became fascinated by the concept that there are reasons why people do what they do and feel what they feel. This morphed into a lifelong desire to understand what makes people tick and then developed into a vision for my life of helping people live healthy, happy lives emotionally and relationally. I first made this vision a reality through my professional work as a psychotherapist and then later through serving as a recovery ministry leader. I now do this through my writing. Though the methods I employed to make this vision a reality in the world differed, the vision remained constant.

In summary, if you have a vision for your life, something you want to achieve or create, you will either give birth to it or be miserable. It's like the feeling a pregnant woman has right at the end of her pregnancy when she wants to scream out loud "Get this baby out of me!" (speaking from personal experience). No one else can make that vision a reality because no one else has the same mix of life experiences and personality characteristics that you have. More importantly, no one else has the passion the vision evokes.

2. Passion

Passion is the feeling that accompanies the vision; it's what energizes you to make the vision a reality.

Though I have always been passionate about helping people live healthy, happy lives emotionally and relationally, that passion exploded and consumed me when God called me to be a Celebrate Recovery ministry leader. I experienced this passion as a driving force inside me that felt like hurricane force winds pushing me in the direction of making God's call on my life a reality in the world. *NOTHING* was going to stop me.

It was this passion that held me steadfast in the face of fierce opposition.

3. Internal motivation

Internal motivation can also be described as self-discipline. Someone who is internally motivated does not need anyone else to tell him or her what to do or when to do it. The impetus for action comes from inside. It comes from the vision and the passion the vision evokes.

4. Focus

The kind of focus needed to make the vision a reality in the world requires an ability and willingness to say no to anything that is a distraction. It's a laser focus.

"The power of focusing can be seen in light. Diffused light has little power or impact, but you can concentrate its energy by focusing it. With a magnifying glass, the rays of the sun can be focused to set grass or paper on fire. When light is focused even more as a laser beam, it can cut through steel."[126]

Jesus had this type of laser focus. He understood that the ultimate purpose for which he had come to earth was to offer himself as a sacrifice for all the sins and wrongdoings of all humankind. Throughout the three years of his earthly ministry, Jesus never lost sight of his purpose. As he went about ministering to people by teaching them and healing them, he was always moving toward the fulfillment of his ultimate purpose. "Jesus went through the towns and villages, teaching as he went, always pressing on toward Jerusalem" (Luke 13:22).

5. Teachable

As described in chapter three, Bruce was teachable.

- "Weekends I spent at the local CYO, YMCA or high school dances . . . I was silent, inscrutable, arms folded, standing in front of the lead guitarist of whatever band was playing, watching every move his fingers made."
- He and Steve traveled to that café many times to watch and listen to bands, learning from them.
- "I figured if I didn't have a voice, I was going to really need to write, perform and use what voice I had to its fullest ability. I was going to have to learn all the tricks, singing from your chest, singing from your abdomen, singing from your throat, great phrasing, timing and dynamics . . . I studied everyone who I loved who sounded real to me, whose voices excited me and touched my heart."

Becky was also teachable. As described in chapter nine, she recognized her need to learn to be a better manager when she moved into the full-time position of business manager at the publishing company and sought out people to teach her. She again recognized a need to learn as she was getting the clothing giveaway off the ground and again sought out people to teach her.

6. Risk taking

Taking a risk requires courage. Contrary to what some might think, courage is not the absence of fear. Courage is doing what you are afraid to do while you are still afraid to do it. Courage is not letting fear control you or rule you.

Fear of failure is one obstacle to risk taking. Here's the thing, though: failure does not have to mean the death of your dream, the end of your vision. It can simply be part of the process, a learning experience, one step along the way. John Maxwell has this to say about fear of failure: "If you really want to achieve your dreams—I mean *really* achieve them, not just daydream or talk about them—you've got to get out there and fail. Fail early, fail often, but always fail forward. Turn your mistakes into stepping-stones for success."[127]

Howard Schultz has this to say about taking risks: "Whatever you do, don't play it safe. Don't do things the way they've always been done. Don't try to fit the system. If you do what's expected of you, you'll never accomplish more than others expect."[128]

When it became clear that Jerry Baldwin and Gordon Bowker were not going to share his vision for the future of Starbucks, he needed to decide whether to stay at Starbucks and let go of his vision or leave and strike out on his own. He chose to take the road less traveled, the risky road.

7. Willingness to do whatever it takes

Nothing worthwhile is ever easy, short, or quick. Turning a vision into a reality in the world is invariably going to take longer and cost more than you imagined. An example of Bruce's willingness: "When our recording budget ran dry, I took the Francis Ford Coppola route, busting the piggy bank and spending everything I had. The results were I went broke while recording a lot of good music."[129]

Cost is not always measured in dollars and cents. Since I have been walking in obedience to God's purposes for my life, I have encountered much opposition. Most of the opposition I have encountered has come from religious people. From 2003 until the time of this writing, I have episodically been lied about, betrayed, ostracized, abandoned, and had coup attempts (some successful, some not) organized against me. All of these episodes were orchestrated by religious people. Some were orchestrated by religious leaders. Though these episodes were painful and lonely to live through, not one caused me to doubt God's directives to me. As I looked to God for comfort and strength to get through each episode, my relationship with him deepened and my resolve to obey him strengthened. I drew much comfort from the following words of Jesus in the Sermon on the Mount:

> God blesses you when people mock you and persecute you and lie about you and say all

sorts of evil things against you because you are my followers. Be happy about it! Be very glad! For a great reward awaits you in heaven. And remember, the ancient prophets were persecuted in the same way. (Matthew 5:11–12)

I know that I am far from the only person who has had to pay a price for walking in obedience to God. I also know that the price I have paid is very small in comparison the prices others have paid.

In Paul's second letter to the church in Corinth, he shared with them the price he paid to fulfill the call God placed on his life.

Five different times the Jewish leaders gave me thirty-nine lashes. Three times I was beaten with rods. Once I was stoned. Three times I was shipwrecked. Once I spent a whole night and a day adrift at sea. I have traveled on many long journeys. I have faced danger from rivers and from robbers. I have faced danger from my own people, the Jews, as well as from the Gentiles. I have faced danger in the cities, in the deserts, and on the seas. And I have faced danger from men who claim to be believers but are not. I have worked hard and long, enduring many sleepless nights. I have been hungry and thirsty and have often gone without food. I have shivered in the cold, without enough clothing to keep me warm. (2 Corinthians 11:24–27)

8. Perseverance

The kind of perseverance needed to turn a vision into a reality is an absolute refusal to give up; it is an unwavering determination to not quit until the vision takes tangible shape.

Howard has this to say about perseverance:

> So many times, I've been told it can't be done. Again and again, I've had to use every ounce of perseverance and persuasion I can summon to make things happen. Life is a series of near misses. But a lot of what we ascribe to luck is not luck at all. It's seizing the day and accepting responsibility for your future. It's seeing what other people don't see, and pursuing that vision, no matter who tells you not to . . . when you really believe—in yourself, in your dream—you just have to do everything you possibly can to take control and make your vision a reality. No great achievement happens by luck.[130]

Other individuals who did not give up:

- Abraham Lincoln failed in business three times and lost seven elections before becoming President of the United States.
- Henry Ford failed and went broke five times before he succeeded.
- Thomas Edison was told by a teacher that he was too stupid to learn anything and that he should go into a field where he

might succeed by virtue of his pleasant personality.

- After his first audition Fred Astaire received the following feedback from an MGM executive: "Can't act. Slightly bald. Can dance a little."
- Albert Einstein wasn't able to speak until he was four years old. Teachers said he would never amount to much.
- A so-called football expert once said of two-time Super Bowl winning coach Vince Lombardi: "He possesses minimal football knowledge. Lacks motivation."
- NBA superstar Michael Jordan was cut from his high school basketball team.
- Walt Disney was fired from a newspaper for lacking imagination and having no original ideas.
- The Beatles were rejected by Decca Recording Studio because "We don't like their sound; they have no future in show business."
- Oprah Winfrey was demoted from her job as a news anchor because she "wasn't fit for television."

Individuals close to my heart who did not give up:

- Dr. Seuss's first book was rejected by 27 publishers.
- Stephen King's first novel, *Carrie*, was rejected by 30 publishers.

- *Chicken Soup for the Soul* was rejected 140 times.
- Margaret Mitchell's *Gone with the Wind* was rejected by 38 publishers.
- James Joyce's *Dubliner* was rejected 18 times and took nine years before it reached publication.
- Max Lucado's first book was rejected by 14 publishers.
- J. K. Rowling's first manuscript, *Harry Potter*, was rejected by 12 publishers before one was willing to give her a chance. That publisher, however, told her to get a day job because she had little chance of making money in children's books.

As for myself, the writing and publishing journey has been nothing like I expected it to be. It has taken more perseverance, risk taking, and financial resources than I imagined, *AND* I am not at the end of this journey. I am committed to keep writing, regardless of the cost, until everything God wants me to write is written and published. (If you would like to read about my writing journey in detail, go to Appendix 4.)

CHAPTER ELEVEN

ADDITIONAL ELEMENTS

In addition to all the elements described in the previous chapter, there are two additional characteristics and behaviors that individuals need to manifest if they hope to be successful in fulfilling God's call on their lives. They are:

- Their security is in God, not in anything the world gives.
- They rely on the Holy Spirit to guide and empower them.

1. Security in God.

In his most famous sermon, the Sermon on the Mount, Jesus told us that God will take care of us if we live for him.

> That is why I tell you not to worry about everyday life—whether you have enough food and drink, or enough clothes to wear. Isn't life more than food, and your body more than clothing? Look

159

at the birds. They don't plant or harvest or store food in barns, for your heavenly Father feeds them. And aren't you far more valuable to him than they are? Can all your worries add a single moment to your life?

And why worry about your clothing? Look at the lilies of the field and how they grow. They don't work or make their clothing, yet Solomon in all his glory was not dressed as beautifully as they are. And if God cares so wonderfully for wildflowers that are here today and thrown into the fire tomorrow, he will certainly care for you. Why do you have so little faith?

So don't worry about these things, saying, "What will we eat? What we will drink? What will we wear?" These things dominate the thoughts of unbelievers, but your heavenly Father already knows all your needs. Seek the Kingdom of God above all else, and live righteously, and he will give you everything you need. (Matthew 6:25–33)

Personal Note: As I mentioned in chapter six, this Scripture passage was instrumental in my journey to obedience. As I read these words over and over day after day, they slowly took root in me and I began to believe them. My faith and trust that God would take care of me and provide for me grew in direct proportion to my belief in these words.

Later in that sermon, Jesus again made the point that God will take care of his children: "'You parents—if your children ask for a loaf of bread, do you give them a stone instead? Or if they ask for a fish, do you give them a snake? Of course not! So if you sinful people know how to give good gifts to your children, how much more will your heavenly Father give good gifts to those who ask him'" (Matthew 7:9–11).

When speaking to a young man he met on the road, Jesus once again made the point that our trust must be in God, not in the things of the world:

> As Jesus was starting out on his way to Jerusalem, a man came running up to him, knelt down, and asked, "Good Teacher, what must I do to inherit eternal life?"
>
> "Why do you call me good?" Jesus asked. "Only God is truly good. But to answer your question, you know the commandments: 'You must not murder. You must not commit adultery. You must not steal. You must not testify falsely. You must not cheat anyone. Honor your father and mother.'"
>
> "Teacher," the man replied, "I've obeyed all these commandments since I was young."
>
> Looking at the man, Jesus felt genuine love for him. "There is still one thing you haven't done," he told him. "Go and sell all your possessions and give the money to the poor, and you will have treasure in heaven. Then come, follow me."
>
> At this the man's face fell, and he went away sad, for he had many possessions. (Mark 10:17–23)

The young man's unwillingness to sell his possessions and follow Jesus clearly indicates that he valued his possessions more than he valued a relationship with Jesus. He placed his security and trust in his possessions, his material wealth, not in Jesus. In fact, I believe this is exactly why Jesus asked him to sell his possessions—Jesus wanted to see where the man's heart was.

The importance of trusting God for one's security rather than trusting the things of the world continued to be taught long after Jesus's earthly ministry ended. Paul taught this to the churches he planted, and his words hold true for us today as well.

In his first letter to Timothy, pastor of the church in Ephesus, Paul said: "Teach those who are rich in this world not to be proud and not to trust in their money, which is so unreliable. Their trust should be in God, who richly gives us all we need for our enjoyment" (1 Timothy 6:17). In his first letter to the church in Corinth, he said: "Those who use the things of the world should not become attached to them. For this world as we know it will soon pass away" (1 Corinthians 7:31).

Note: Paul did not say it is bad to be rich. He also did not say that we shouldn't have or use the things of the world. He said we are not to become *attached* to our money or our things and are not to place our trust in them.

James, the half-brother of Jesus, also taught this. He wrote about what happens to those who have not fully placed their faith and trust in God:

If you need wisdom, ask our generous God, and he will give it to you. He will not rebuke you for asking. But when you ask him, be sure that your faith is in God alone. Do not waver, for a person with divided loyalty is as unsettled as a wave of the sea that is blown and tossed by the wind. Such people should not expect to receive anything from the Lord. Their loyalty is divided between God and the world, and they are unstable in everything they do. (James 1:5–8)

2. Reliance on the Holy Spirit.

At various times during his earthly ministry, Jesus spoke to the apostles and disciples about the Holy Spirit. Before he sent the twelve apostles on their first mission trip, he told them about the role the Holy Spirit would play in their lives and in their ministries:

> You will stand trial before governors and kings because you are my followers. But this will be your opportunity to tell the rulers and other unbelievers about me. When you are arrested, don't worry about how to respond or what to say. God will give you the right words at the right time. For it is not you who will be speaking—it will be the Spirit of your Father speaking through you. (Matthew 10:18–20)

During the last meal he shared with them prior to his death, he again spoke to them about the Holy Spirit.

> If you love me, obey my commandments. And I will ask the Father, and he will give you another

Advocate, who will never leave you. He is the Holy Spirit, who leads into all truth. The world cannot receive him, because it isn't looking for him, and doesn't recognize him. But you know him, because he lives with you now and later will be in you. (John 14:15–17)

During the times he appeared to his disciples following his crucifixion and resurrection from the dead, he continued to talk with them about the Holy Spirit. "Once when he was eating with them, he commanded them, 'Do not leave Jerusalem until the Father sends you the gift he promised, as I told you before. John baptized with water, but in just a few days you will be baptized with the Holy Spirit'" (Acts 1:4–5).

Immediately prior to his ascension into heaven, Jesus spoke to his disciples one last time about the Holy Spirit. He told them, "'You will receive power when the Holy Spirit comes upon you. And you will be my witnesses, telling people about me everywhere—in Jerusalem, throughout Judea, in Samaria, and to the ends of the earth'" (Acts 1:8).

As Jesus promised, the Holy Spirit came to the apostles and disciples soon after Jesus ascended into heaven.

On the day of Pentecost all the believers were meeting together in one place. Suddenly, there was a sound from heaven like the roaring of a mighty windstorm, and it filled the house where they were sitting. Then, what looked like flames or tongues of fire appeared and settled on each of them. And everyone present was filled with the Holy Spirit and began speaking in other languages, as the Holy Spirit gave them this ability. (Acts 2:1–4)

Peter then went outside and spoke to the crowd gathered there: "People of Israel, listen! God publicly endorsed Jesus the Nazarene by doing powerful miracles, wonders, and signs through him, as you well know. But God knew what would happen, and his prearranged plan was carried out when Jesus was betrayed. With the help of lawless Gentiles, you nailed him to a cross and killed him. But God released him from the horrors of death and raised him back to life, for death could not keep him in its grip." (Acts 2:22–24)

"God raised Jesus from the dead, and we are all witnesses of this. Now he is exalted to the place of highest honor in heaven, at God's right hand. And the Father, as he had promised, gave him the Holy Spirit to pour out upon us, just as you see and hear today." (Acts 2:32–33)

Peter then went on to say that the gift of the Holy Spirit is promised to all who become followers of Jesus. Once they were empowered by the Holy Spirit, Peter and the other apostles and disciples began to carry on Jesus's work in Jerusalem, ministering in his name. They did not let opposition, including arrest, stop them.

The apostles were performing many miraculous signs and wonders among the people . . . More and more people believed and were brought to the Lord—crowds of both men and women. As a result of the apostles' work, sick people were brought out into the streets on beds and mats so that Peter's shadow might fall across some of them as he went by. Crowds came from the villages around Jerusalem, bringing their sick and those possessed by evil spirits, and they were all healed. (Acts 5:12, 14–16)

Paul also relied on the Holy Spirit's power to fulfill his God-given assignment. In his second letter to the church in Corinth, he told them,

We don't go around preaching about ourselves. We preach that Jesus Christ is Lord, and we ourselves are your servants for Jesus' sake. For God, who said, "Let there be light in the darkness," has made this light shine in our hearts so we could know the glory of God that is seen in the face of Jesus Christ.

We now have this light shining in our hearts, but we ourselves are like fragile clay jars containing this great treasure. This makes it clear that our great power is from God, not from ourselves. (2 Corinthians 4:5–7)

In his letter to the church in Colosse, Paul made his dependence on God explicitly clear: "That's why I work and struggle so hard, depending on Christ's mighty power that works within me" (Colossians 1:29).

What about us? What about now?

When Peter said that the gift of the Holy Spirit is promised to all who become followers of Jesus, he was not only speaking to those who were listening to him on the day of Pentecost; he was speaking to all believers throughout time.

Paul said the same thing to the church in Ephesus, to the church in Galatia, and to us: "When you believed in Christ, he identified you as his own by giving you the Holy Spirit, whom he promised long ago" (Ephesians 1:13); "Let me ask you this one question: Did you receive the Holy Spirit by obeying the law of Moses? Of course not! You received the Spirit because you believed the message you heard about Christ" (Galatians 3:2).

When we give our life to Jesus, God's Spirit, the Holy Spirit, comes to live inside us. We then have the opportunity to let the Spirit transform us from the inside out to become more like Jesus. "Let the Spirit renew your thoughts and attitudes" (Ephesians 4:23). This does not happen overnight. It is a process that occurs over time and requires our cooperation. The Spirit molds us, much as a potter molds clay, or chisels away at us, much as a sculptor chisels a piece of stone.

As we cooperate with God's Spirit, our ungodly thoughts and behaviors are slowly transformed into godly thoughts and behaviors until we eventually, hopefully, develop a character that mirrors that of Jesus. During this process, it is important to remember to be kind to oneself. Old habits die hard. They don't give up without a fight, and the more ingrained they are the harder they fight.

As we cooperate with the Spirit, we gradually turn over more and more parts of ourselves and our lives to God, until we are eventually able to give ourselves and our lives to him completely. "Since we are living by the Spirit, let us follow the Spirit's leading in every part of our lives" (Galatians 5:25).

How does the Spirit lead us?

Sometimes he leads us with internal promptings that won't go away, no matter how much we ignore them or try to rationalize our way out of doing whatever it is we are being prompted to do. An example of this is when I started sensing that God wanted me to step out of my profession as a psychotherapist. I didn't want to do this, so I tried to negotiate with him and wrestled with him for about one and a half years. The feeling kept getting stronger, until I could no longer ignore it, and I finally resigned from my position and stepped out of my profession.

Another way he has led me is by having words jump off a page as I read the Bible. He did this in 2004, when the last two verses of 1 Chronicles 28 jumped off the page at me, confirming that he did want me to lead that Celebrate Recovery ministry.

He has also led me by instilling in me a strong emotional response as I listened to a worship song. He has also chosen to speak to me at times through people.

The telltale mark that confirms to me that I am following the Spirit's leading is the abundance of internal peace and joy I feel when I do what he is leading me to do. When I do not follow the Spirit's leading, i.e., when I am outside God's will in some area of my life, I am anxious, depressed, sad, restless, and/or agitated—anything but peaceful. This motivates me to get back on track with God and walk in his will. When I do, he once again fills me with peace and joy.

The Spirit not only leads us, he empowers us, just as he empowered Peter, Paul, and the other apostles and disciples. Sam Hunter, in his book *The Missing Link*, describes how the Holy Spirit empowers us:

> The Holy Spirit works within our actions but beyond our powers. He seems to mix his power with our efforts . . . the Spirit moves within and through your efforts, beyond what we could accomplish on our own—within our actions, but beyond our powers . . . Step by step, we are laid hold of by a movement, a power, a Spirit greater than ourselves, who expands our energies and our efforts beyond our own power . . .
>
> Jesus likened the Spirit to the wind. It blows and we see the results, but we do not see the Spirit—at least not with the eyes in our head. We see the movement of the Spirit with the eyes of our heart . . . We do our part, but the wind of the Spirit powers us—no effort on our part, often no movement by the Spirit, within our actions, beyond our powers.[131]

The internal hurricane force winds I experienced when God called me to be a Celebrate Recovery ministry leader is an example of Holy Spirit power. Without this power linked to the passion my vision evoked, I would not have been able to hold steadfast in the face of the opposition I experienced.

Suggestion: If you are finding it difficult to change behavior and/or thought patterns, I suggest you work a Christ-centered 12 Step program. It was through working the 12 Steps with Jesus Christ as my Higher Power that I was able to break my approval seeking / people pleasing addiction. Further, I learned how to trust God, how to surrender to him, and how to obey him. I also developed clarity regarding what I can control and what I cannot control. Though the 12 Steps were developed by Bill W. and Dr. Bob as a roadmap or path to recovery when they founded Alcoholics Anonymous in the 1930s, the 12 Steps are not only applicable to drug and/or alcohol problems. They are applicable to any struggle in life.

It is interesting to note that many people believe the 12 Steps were divinely inspired, and, indeed, Bill W. founded Alcoholics Anonymous following a spiritual experience he had in which his desire to drink alcohol was removed. For me, the 12 Steps have proven to be a roadmap to God and guidelines for living a Christian life. (See Appendix 5.)

CHAPTER TWELVE

FREEDOM: RESURRECTION STYLE

Just as success means different things to different people, freedom also means different things to different people. According to dictionary.com, *freedom* is "exemption from external control, interference, or regulation; the power to determine action without restraint." This definition refers to political freedom, secular freedom. Another type of freedom, a totally different kind, is spiritual freedom, resurrection style freedom. Spiritual freedom is being released from one's own internal bonds or restraints.

Political freedom and spiritual freedom are radically different and do not necessarily coexist. It is possible to be politically free and be in spiritual bondage. It is also possible to be spiritually free and be in political bondage. Political freedom is being released from the bonds of others. Spiritual freedom is being released from the bonds of self. In short, political freedom depends on external circumstances; spiritual freedom depends on internal circumstances.

Obtaining freedom, whether it be political freedom or spiritual freedom, involves cost and sacrifice. Political freedom will be discussed first.

America's journey to freedom

The United States declared its political freedom from England in 1776 with the writing and signing of the Declaration of Independence. Excerpt:

> We hold these truths to be self-evident, that all men are created equal, that they are endowed by their Creator with certain unalienable rights, that among these are life, liberty, and the pursuit of happiness. That, to secure these rights, governments are instituted among men, deriving their just powers from the consent of the governed. That, whenever any form of government becomes destructive of these ends, it is the right of the people to alter or to abolish it, and to institute new government, laying its foundation on such principles, and organizing its powers in such form, as to them shall seem most likely to effect their safety and happiness.

Though the American colonists declared their freedom from England, King George III didn't just hand it to them. The colonists had to fight for it (the American Revolution), and they had to win the fight, which they did. The colonists paid a steep price to obtain their freedom from England. The price the colonists paid included:

- Military casualties were approximately 50,000 men.
- Of these 50,000, approximately 8,000 died in battle and 17,000 died from disease.
- Of the 17,000 who died from disease, 8–12 thousand of these contracted diseases while living in prison ships in New York harbor.
- Another 2,500 Americans died while encamped at Valley Forge in the winter of 1777–1778.

As a result of the American colonies winning their War for Independence from England, *WHITE MEN* were able to exercise political freedom. As white women were not allowed to vote, they had no avenue with which to exercise political freedom. As African American men and women were held in slavery by white slave owners in many states, they did not benefit at all by the colonists winning their War for Independence. Another war needed to be fought, Americans against Americans (the Civil War), almost a century later for them to be released from slavery. Another steep price was paid for the abolition of slavery:

- Military casualties were approximately 750,000 soldier deaths.
- Of those 750,000 men, 56,000 died in prisons.
- Another 60,000 men lost limbs.

Though slaves were legally set free at the end of the Civil War with the signing of the Emancipation Proclamation in 1865, they were not able to actually exercise their political freedom and civil rights. Much legislation and social activism were needed to accomplish that.

In 1868 the Fourteenth Amendment to the Constitution was adopted. This amendment granted citizenship to "all persons born or naturalized in the United States." This included former slaves who had been recently freed. In addition, the amendment forbids states from denying any person "life, liberty or property, without due process of law" or to "deny to any person within its jurisdiction the equal protection of the laws." It still did not, however, guarantee black citizens the ability to exercise their political and civil rights. Still more legislation was needed for that.

In 1870 Congress adopted the Fifteenth Amendment to the Constitution, which prohibits federal and state governments from denying *MEN* the right to vote due to "race, color, or previous condition of servitude." It did not, however, challenge the authority of states and localities to establish and administer their own voting requirements, and many southern states did exactly that. They used various methods, such as literacy tests, poll taxes, intimidation, threats, and violence to keep people of color from voting. White men who could not pass the literacy test or pay the poll tax were permitted to vote under grandfather clauses.

In addition to the discriminatory practices at the polls, local and state laws in southern states, known as Jim Crow laws, banned blacks from schools, public restrooms, lunch counters, theaters, trains, etc. The civil rights movement that took place in the 1950s and 1960s changed this.

Price paid to exercise political freedom

The civil rights movement was successful in integrating public facilities and getting black men the right to vote. Civil rights workers did this through civil disobedience (direct action through nonviolent resistance). Some nonviolent strategies they used were boycotts, sit-ins, and marches. Example: In Montgomery, Alabama, blacks boycotted buses for over one year ('55–'56). This resulted in the buses in Montgomery being integrated.

Though the acts of civil disobedience were nonviolent, many of them resulted in violent episodes due to law enforcement officers (many of whom were members of the Ku Klux Klan) routinely using night sticks, billy clubs, attack dogs, city fire hoses, and tear gas to force unarmed protesters into submission. This resulted in the deaths of *MANY* southern black men, women, and children. In addition, northerners who traveled to the South to help blacks register to vote were murdered by segregationists. White supremacists also bombed black schools, churches, businesses, and residences.

One group of northerners who were particularly courageous and selfless were the Freedom Riders. Freedom Riders were interracial groups of people who boarded buses in the North that were heading for the South. White riders would sit in the back of the bus and black riders in the front. At rest stops, the white people would go into black only areas and the black people would go into white only areas. Over a six-month period in 1961 more than 60 Freedom Rides rolled through the South.

Freedom Riders were treated very harshly by Southern law enforcement officers. In Birmingham, the Public Safety commissioner gave KKK members 15 minutes to attack an incoming group of Freedom Riders before allowing the police to protect them. The riders were severely beaten, and one man (a white civil rights activist) required 50 stitches in his head. All over the South hundreds of freedom riders were jailed and were then treated very harshly in jail, crammed into tiny, filthy cells and sporadically beaten.

The Freedom Rides, and the violent reactions they provoked, bolstered the credibility of the Civil Rights Movement. They called national attention to the way law enforcement officers in the South disregarded federal laws and used violence to enforce local Jim Crow laws. In addition, the fact that Freedom Riders were northerners who faced danger on behalf of southern blacks impressed many blacks throughout the South and inspired them to engage in direct action for civil rights. They then formed the backbone of the wider civil rights movement, which eventually led to the passage of the Civil Rights Act of 1964, which banned discrimination based on race, color, religion, or national origin in employment practices and in public facilities.

Though the Civil Rights Act was most definitely landmark legislation, it did not remove the obstacles black men encountered at the polls, as it still did not forbid states and localities from establishing and administering their own voting requirements. It also did not pave the way for black women to vote.

Civil rights workers again stepped up to the plate with their uncommon courage and limitless perseverance and were able to influence legislators to pass the Voting Rights Act of 1965, which prohibited state and local governments from imposing any voting law that resulted in discrimination against racial or language minorities. It also contained a provision prohibiting certain jurisdictions from implementing any change affecting voting without receiving preapproval from the US Attorney General or the US District Court for the District of Colombia. Further, it gave black voters legal means to challenge voting restrictions and specifically allowed black women to vote. Obtaining the right to vote for women, especially black women, was a long time coming and involved much cost and sacrifice.

Cost of obtaining political freedom for women

Women's suffrage in the United States was achieved gradually at state and local levels during the late 19th and early 20th centuries. It culminated in 1920 with the passage of the 19th Amendment to the Constitution, which gave *WHITE* women the right to vote.

In 1848 Elizabeth Stanton emerged as a women's suffrage leader. Her strong opinions not only made her unpopular with men; they also made her unpopular with many women. In 1851 she met Susan B. Anthony, and the two women formed a strong and formidable partnership in the effort to secure the right to vote for women.

Suffragists promoted swimming competitions, scaled mountains, piloted airplanes, and staged large-scale parades to gain publicity. In 1912 they organized a 12-day, 170-mile hike from New York City to Albany. In 1913 they marched 225 miles from Newark to Washington in 16 days, with numerous photo opportunities and press interviews along the way. This gained them a national audience. In 1917 they formed the National Women's Party, an organization that fought for women's right to vote on the same terms as men by lobbying for a constitutional amendment ensuring women's suffrage.

The movement slowly gained support, and as it did white suffragists realized they could gain even more support if they excluded black women, so they began to marginalize as many black women as possible. One way they did this was by promoting the concept of the "educated suffragist," i.e., that a woman needed to be educated to vote. Since primarily only white women were educated, this effectively shut black women out of the suffragist movement.

World War I provided the final push for women's suffrage in America. After President Woodrow Wilson announced that World War I was a war for democracy, women were up in arms. The National Women's Party picketed outside the White House and engaged in a series of protests against the Wilson administration. Wilson ignored the protests for six months, but on June 20, 1917, as a Russian delegation drove up to the White House, suffragettes unfurled a banner stating, "We women of America tell you that America is not a democracy. Twenty million women are denied the right to vote." Another banner on August 14, 1917, referred to "Kaiser Wilson" and compared the plight of the German people with that of American women.

As a result of these actions, many women were arrested, and many were jailed. In October one of the women in jail began a hunger strike. President Wilson then finally changed his position and began to advocate for women's suffrage. The Nineteenth Amendment to the Constitution, giving *WHITE WOMEN* the right to vote, was finally passed in 1920.

When black women were excluded from the benefits of the Nineteenth Amendment, they did not passively sit back and wait to see whether they were going to be allowed to vote. They actively tried to register to vote. In all parts of the United States, they came up against various methods aimed at stopping them from voting. These methods included having to wait in line for up to 12 hours to register, pay head taxes, and take new tests. One of the new tests required them to read and interpret the Constitution. In the South, black women faced even more severe obstacles to voting. These obstacles included bodily harm and fabricated charges designed to land them in jail if they attempted to vote. This went on until 1965, when the Voting Rights Act was signed into law.

Once the right to vote was obtained for *all* women, the women's movement moved into its second phase (1960s to 1990s). This phase focused on procuring additional civil and human rights for women and resulted in:

- marital rape laws.
- establishment of rape crisis centers and battered women's shelters.
- changes in custody and divorce laws.
- equal pay for equal work standards.
- equal credit opportunities.
- establishment of a law requiring US military academies to accept women.

- integration of the military academies, the armed forces, NASA, single sex colleges, men's clubs, and the Supreme Court.

Obtaining spiritual freedom

As described above, our political freedoms were obtained by the prices paid by countless men and women. Our spiritual freedom, however, was paid for by the price one man paid. That man was Jesus Christ. We obtain spiritual freedom when we place our trust in him, accept his death on the cross as a personal gift, and surrender our life to him to do with as he pleases.

At the beginning of his earthly ministry, Jesus preached in the synagogue in Nazareth, his hometown. He read the following words of Isaiah the prophet: "'The Spirit of the Lord is upon me, for he has anointed me to bring Good News to the poor. He has sent me to proclaim that captives will be released, that the blind will see, that the oppressed will be set free'" (Luke 4:18). He then stated, "'The Scripture you've just heard has been fulfilled this very day!'" (Luke 4:21). By claiming that he was the fulfillment of Isaiah's prophecy, he was stating publicly that he was the long-awaited Messiah.

Throughout the three years of his earthly ministry, Jesus set people free from all kinds of physical disabilities, handicaps, and illnesses; from demonic possession; and even from death. His final and ultimate acts of setting people free were his crucifixion and resurrection from the dead.

By dying on the cross, Jesus gave us the gift of a personal relationship with God. If we choose to accept this gift and make Jesus the Lord of our lives, we become part of God's family. Our relationship with him then lasts throughout our life on earth and extends into and throughout our life in eternity.

As discussed in the previous chapter, the Holy Spirit comes to live inside us when we give our life to Jesus. The Spirit then transforms us from the inside out to become more like Jesus. If we let him, the Spirit will set us free from anything that hinders us from becoming who we were created to be. He then empowers us to do what we were created to do. Therein lies true freedom, resurrection style freedom.

In his letter to the church in Rome, Paul tells us that the same power that enabled Jesus to rise from the dead is available to us. "Just as Christ was raised from the dead by the glorious power of the Father, now we also may live new lives" (Romans 6:4). "The Spirit of God, who raised Jesus from the dead, lives in you. And just as God raised Christ Jesus from the dead, he will give life to your mortal bodies by this same Spirit living within you" (Romans 8:11). This is the abundant life Jesus referred to.

To summarize:

- We enjoy the benefits of political freedom by winning.
- We enjoy the benefits of spiritual freedom by surrendering.
- When we are politically free, we do what we want, within the bounds of law.
- When we are spiritually free, we do what God wants.

- There is nothing we need to do to enjoy our political freedom.
- There are three things we need to do to enjoy our spiritual freedom.
    1. Accept Jesus's work on the cross as a personal gift.
    2. Give our life to him to do with as he pleases.
    3. Cooperate with the Holy Spirit to heal any emotional wounds, destructive habits, or unhealthy thoughts that inhibit us from becoming who God created us to be.

I would like to leave you with some words from Jeremy Camp's worship song "Same Power":

I can walk down this dark and painful road
I can free every fear of the unknown
I can hear all God's children singing out
We will not be overtaken; we will not be overcome
The same power that rose Jesus from the grave
The same power that commands the dead to wake
Lives in us, lives in us.

EPILOGUE

Most of this book was written while I was staying at home during the 2020 coronavirus pandemic. Though I had started writing it long before any of us heard of coronavirus, I frequently let life get in the way of writing. When circumstances were such that life as I knew it could no longer get in the way, I settled in and finished it.

Don't get me wrong, though; this was not a smooth process. There were times when I, like many others on the planet, let irritability, restlessness, and anxiety get in the way of productivity. During those times I would wallow in my feelings for a while and then eventually implement a course correction by reminding myself that I and everyone I love was healthy. This provided the impetus I needed to make the necessary attitude adjustment and get back to writing.

Writing, for me, is a time of reflecting and clarifying thoughts, feelings, beliefs, and goals. It is also a time of learning. As I do the needed research for a book, I am constantly learning. This time of writing proved to be no exception. Researching and writing the stories of the individuals I chose to share nurtured my spirit, as I stated in the introduction.

- Howard encourages me to stay true to my vision, to listen to my passion, and to take the needed risks to make the vision a reality in the world.
- Bruce encourages me to do whatever it takes to make the vision a reality.
- Theodore encourages me to not be afraid to make course corrections.
- Peter comforts and affirms me. I have a personality much like Peter's. I can be impetuous and impulsive, jumping out of the boat before considering possible consequences of my actions. My mouth also frequently starts moving before my brain is fully in gear.
- Paul inspires me. He stayed true to his God-given purpose in spite of extremely difficult and painful consequences.
- Becky reminds me to slow down long enough to seek God and to listen for his voice before embarking on a course of action.
- Jackie challenges me to consistently live my life for an audience of One, regardless of whether the people around me agree with what I am doing.

As I have hopefully made clear, I have benefitted from writing this book. I truly hope you have benefitted by reading it.

ADDENDUM

Between the writing and editing phases of this book, the Black Lives Matter movement exploded, sparked by the murder of George Floyd while in police custody in Minneapolis.

It is heartbreakingly sad to acknowledge that controversy over racial equality has been present in America since we were a British colony and, obviously, is still present. The original draft of the Declaration of Independence included a clause abolishing slavery. This clause caused fierce debate between the northern and southern delegates to the Continental Congress. Prior to the vote on whether to accept the resolution for independence, delegations from some of the southern states made it known that they would vote no if the clause to abolish slavery remained in the document. Since all thirteen colonies needed to vote yes for the resolution to pass, Thomas Jefferson, with much regret, removed it.

Though I understand that at times it is necessary to lose a battle to win a war, removing the clause to abolish slavery insured that racial inequality was inextricably woven into the fabric of the United States. Two hundred twenty-four years later it is still there, and it is still being fiercely debated. Due to the actions taken and sacrifices made by countless individuals though, it is not woven into our fabric as tightly.

In spite of the tremendous legislative strides made since the signing of the Emancipation Proclamation in 1865, racism still exists. It exists because racism is not a legal condition, it is a heart condition, and legislation does not change hearts. Racism will be removed from our country's fabric completely when hearts change to the point where we are all color blind, seeing each other as people, not white people or black people or brown people or yellow people. Hearts will change when the evil of racism is confronted directly and openly.

It is impossible to know in advance what the ripple effect will be of any action we take or fail to take. I highly doubt Rosa Parks had any idea of how far the ripples would go when she refused to give her seat on a Montgomery city bus to a white passenger on December 1, 1955.

Helen Keller once said, "I cannot do everything, but I can do something. I will not refuse to do the something I can do." Not everyone will participate in a major social movement however, everyone can do something, and maybe all these somethings together will move us closer to racial equality in the United States.

APPENDIX ONE

"That is why I tell you not to worry about everyday life—whether you have enough food and drink, or enough clothes to wear. Isn't life more than food, and your body more than clothing? Look at the birds. They don't plant or harvest or store food in barns, for your heavenly Father feeds them. And aren't you far more valuable to him than they are? Can all your worries add a single moment to your life?

"And why worry about your clothing? Look at the lilies of the field and how they grow. They don't work or make their clothing, yet Solomon in all his glory was not dressed as beautifully as they are. And if God cares so wonderfully for wildflowers that are here today and thrown into the fire tomorrow, he will certainly care for you. Why do you have so little faith?

"So don't worry about these things, saying, What will we eat? What we will drink? What will we wear? These things dominate the thoughts of unbelievers, but your heavenly Father already knows all your needs. Seek the Kingdom of God above all else, and live righteously, and he will give you everything you need." (Matthew 6:25–33)

APPENDIX TWO

The night before Peter was to be placed on trial, he was asleep, fastened with two chains between two soldiers. Others stood guard at the prison gate. Suddenly, there was a bright light in the cell, and an angel of the Lord stood before Peter. The angel struck him on the side to awaken him and said, "Quick! Get up!" And the chains fell off his wrists. Then the angel told him, "Get dressed and put on your sandals." And he did. "Now put on your coat and follow me," the angel ordered.

So Peter left the cell, following the angel. But all the time he thought it was a vision. He didn't realize it was actually happening. They passed the first and second guard posts and came to the iron gate leading to the city, and this opened for them all by itself. So they passed through and started walking down the street, and then the angel suddenly left him.

Peter finally came to his senses. "It's really true!" he said. "The Lord has sent his angel and saved me from Herod and from what the Jewish leaders had planned to do to me!" (Acts 12:6–11)

APPENDIX THREE

As he was approaching Damascus on this mission, a light from heaven suddenly shone down around him. He fell to the ground and heard a voice saying to him, "Saul! Saul! Why are you persecuting me?"

"Who are you, lord?" Saul asked.

And the voice replied, "I am Jesus, the one you are persecuting! Now get up and go into the city, and you will be told what you must do."

The men with Saul stood speechless, for they heard the sound of someone's voice but saw no one! Saul picked himself up off the ground, but when he opened his eyes he was blind. So his companions led him by the hand to Damascus. He remained there blind for three days and did not eat or drink.

Now there was a believer in Damascus named Ananias. The Lord spoke to him in a vision, calling, "Ananias!"

"Yes, Lord!" he replied.

The Lord said, "Go over to Straight Street, to the house of Judas. When you get there, ask for a man from Tarsus named Saul. He is praying to me right now. I have shown him a vision of a man named Ananias coming in and laying hands on him so he can see again."

"But Lord," exclaimed Ananias, "I've heard many people talk about the terrible things this man has done to the believers in Jerusalem! And he is authorized by the leading priests to arrest everyone who calls upon your name."

But the Lord said, "Go, for Saul is my chosen instrument to take my message to the Gentiles and to kings, as well as to the people of Israel. And I will show him how much he must suffer for my name's sake."

So Ananias went and found Saul. He laid his hands on him and said, "Brother Saul, the Lord Jesus, who appeared to you on the road, has sent me so that you might regain your sight and be filled with the Holy Spirit." Instantly something like scales fell from Saul's eyes, and he regained his sight. Then he got up and was baptized. Afterward he ate some food and regained his strength. (Acts 9:3–19)

APPENDIX FOUR

My writing journey began in 2005, when God called me to write a book about how Celebrate Recovery had helped me overcome multiple hurts, habits, and hang-ups I struggled with as a result of having grown up in an unhealthy family. The result was *When Therapy Isn't Enough*.

As I was writing that book, I was simultaneously reaching out to literary agents and to traditional publishing companies. As I received rejection after rejection, if I heard back from anyone at all, I quickly and painfully learned that no literary agent was going to take me on as a client and no traditional publishing company was going to publish my work because I was a complete unknown. I had no name recognition. So I turned to self-publishing.

A local company, House to House Publications, published the first edition of *When Therapy Isn't Enough* in 2008. In 2011, Tate Publishing Company published a second edition of it. My next book, *When Religion Isn't Enough*, was published by Tate in 2012. *When Religion Isn't Enough* chronicles my journey from religion to relationship, explaining the difference between having religion and having a personal relationship with God.

I then wrote *When the Glass Ceiling Is Stained*. This book was birthed in an experience I had in which I was removed from a church leadership position I firmly believed God had called me to. It discusses the differences between ordination and anointing, as well as the differences between leading and managing. I decided to share this experience and the lessons I learned from it in the hope that other women would benefit from it.

I served in leadership in various Celebrate Recovery ministries for 10 years. In 2013 I had both of my knees replaced (one in June and one in October) and stepped out of the Celebrate Recovery leadership role I was serving in at that time, believing that this season of my life had come to an end. Throughout the following winter (as my knees were healing) I waited on God to let me know what he wanted me to do next and wrote *When Doing Isn't Enough*, published by Tate in 2015.

God did indeed let me know what he wanted me to do next. In July 2014 he lit a fire in my heart to help his daughters be set free from belief systems and practices that reinforce the inequality of the sexes. In response to that fire being lit, I wrote *When Going with the Flow Isn't Enough*, incorporating much of *Glass Ceiling* into it.

As I worked with Tate Publishing Company during the publishing process of *Doing*, I saw a number of red flags that made me uneasy about continuing my relationship with them. Therefore, as I was writing *Going with the Flow*, I began to look for another publishing company and found Credo House Publishers. Credo published *Going with the Flow* in 2017.

Also in 2017 Tate Publishing Company went bankrupt. Before they went out of business, they offered to sell a print-ready file of each of an author's manuscripts to the author for a small fee. I purchased the print-ready file for *Doing* and had Credo re-publish it. *Glass Ceiling* had already been incorporated into *Going with the Flow*, *AND* I decided to write one new manuscript from my first two, *Therapy* and *Religion*. Though the new book is titled *When Therapy Isn't Enough*, it is very different (and better, if I do say so myself) than the earlier book of the same title.

APPENDIX FIVE

Step 1—We admitted that we were powerless over our addictions and compulsive behaviors, that our lives had become unmanageable—is an invitation to face reality and admit that our life isn't working. We stop pretending that it IS working, we admit our powerlessness, and we stop trying to manage our life OUR way. The idea of taking this first step can be overwhelming until we stop looking at our lives through the lens of DENIAL and start seeing them through the lens of reality.

Important note to those who believe that once we accept Christ as our Lord and Savior we are a new being: Our proclamation that "I am a born again Christian; my past is washed clean; I am a new creature; Christ has totally changed me" is true. Our spirits are born again. Our flesh, however, is holding on to a lifetime of hurts, habits, and hang-ups. We need more than salvation. We need transformation. To over-spiritualize the initial work of salvation may be to deny the actual condition of our lives.

Step 1, if worked properly, leaves us feeling empty and ready for Step 2—We came to believe that a power greater than ourselves could restore us to sanity. When we begin to see that help is available to us and as we reach out and accept what our Higher Power has to offer, we start to feel hopeful that our life will improve and we'll feel better. To take this step we need not understand what lies ahead. We need to trust that God knows what lies ahead and that he loves us and will take care of us.

Taking Step 2 positions us to take Step 3—We made a decision to turn our lives and our wills over to the care of God. In the first two steps we became aware of our condition and accepted the idea of a power greater than ourselves. Step 3 is decision time. When we take Step 3, we put God in the driver's seat of our life.

Many of us initially take Step 3 by turning over only certain parts of our lives to God, the problematic parts that are making our lives unmanageable. We hold onto the other parts of our lives, thinking we can manage them just fine, thank you very much. We eventually realize, however, that we cannot barter with God. We must surrender our entire will and every area of our life to his care if we truly want to be free to be who he created us to be. When we are finally able and willing to accept this reality, our journey to wholeness begins for real, and we are ready to work Step 4.

Step 4—We made a searching and fearless moral inventory of ourselves—opens our eyes to the weaknesses in our lives that need changing and helps us to build on our strengths. We examine our behavior and expand our understanding of ourselves. As we begin to see ourselves clearly, we learn to accept our whole character—the good and the bad. As our self-discovery unfolds, we begin to recognize the role that denial has played in our lives. This realization is the basis for embracing the truth of our personal history. An honest and thorough inventory leads to self-acceptance and freedom.

Step 5—We admitted to God, to ourselves, and to another human being the exact nature of our wrongs— gives us the opportunity to set aside our pride as we see ourselves through the lens of reality. Step 5 is a pathway out of isolation and loneliness and results in freedom, happiness, and serenity. Working Step 5 lays a new foundation for our life of relationship to God and commitment to honesty and humility. Our growing relationship with God gives us the courage to examine ourselves and reveals our true self to ourselves, to God, and to another human being. Self-disclosure is an important part of our Christian walk. We were created to live in community with both God and people. Authentic community requires disclosure. It is tempting to believe that telling God is all that is necessary because he ultimately forgives all sins. While this is true, confession to another human being provides special healing and wholeness and releases the grip of hidden sin. Once we share our inventory with God and with another human being, we are ready to move on to Step 6.

Step 6—We were entirely ready to have God remove all these defects of character—provides us with a needed rest as God works in us to create needed change. Our task in this step is to develop the willingness to respond to God's desired action in our lives. We may believe the saying "God helps those who help themselves, so get busy and change." This, however, is not true. Change comes from God, not from our self-will, and it comes when we are willing to Let Go and Let God!

In Step 7—We humbly asked God to remove all our shortcomings—we Let God. We work this step on our knees in humble prayer, asking God to remove our shortcomings, one defect at a time. Asking God to remove our defects is a true measure of our willingness to surrender control. For those of us who have spent our lives thinking we were self-sufficient, surrendering control can be an extremely difficult task. It is also an extremely freeing task. It takes much faith and trust to work this step. We need to remember that God hears us and wants to answer our prayer. We also need to remember that God works on his timetable, not ours. He will remove our defects when he knows we are ready.

Step 8—We made a list of all persons we had harmed and became willing to make amends to them all—begins the process of healing damaged relationships. Up to this point in our recovery, we have been looking at and dealing with how our hurts, habits, and hang-ups have affected us. We now begin to look at how they have harmed others. Reviewing our Fourth Step inventory helps us determine who belongs on our amends list. Once our amends list is done, we are ready to move on to Step 9—We made direct amends to such people whenever possible, except when to do so would have injured them or others.

Step 9 gives us the opportunity to take concrete action to heal the damage of our past and to move further along on the pathway out of isolation and loneliness. Accepting responsibility for the harm we've done to others is a humbling experience because it forces us to admit the effect we have had on people we care about. It requires much courage to successfully complete this step. It is not easy to admit to someone face-to-face that we have hurt him or her and to ask for forgiveness. Doing this, however, leads to increased self-esteem, serenity, and peace, both in ourselves and in our relationships.

Steps 8 and 9 help us repair our past. Step 10—We continued to take personal inventory, and when we were wrong promptly admitted it—is a maintenance step that is designed to help us stay on track in our recovery. Doing a daily inventory and making amends as needed strengthens and protects our recovery and is a vital part of walking a healthy Christian walk.

Step 11—We sought through prayer and meditation to improve our conscious contact with God, praying only for knowledge of His will for us and the power to carry that out—is another maintenance step. Our relationship with God is our most important relationship. In order for that relationship to be vibrant and alive, ongoing honest communication is critical. As we draw near to God in prayer and meditation, we draw close to our source of power, serenity, guidance, and healing. To ignore communication with God is to unplug our power source.

Step 12—Having had a spiritual experience as the result of these steps, we try to carry this message to others and to practice these principles in all our affairs—is an action step. Step 12 calls us to reach out to those who are hurting and struggling, and to share with them our experience, strength, and hope. First Peter 3:10 tells us, "Always be prepared to give an answer to everyone who asks you to give the reason for the hope that you have." The most powerful way we can work Step 12 of carrying this message to others is to actually WALK the Christian walk—to walk the walk, not just talk the talk. When working Step 12, a good rule of thumb is "Actions speak louder than words." There is no more powerful witness of God's transformational love and power than a transformed life that lives that transformation day in and day out.

NOTES

1 Rick Warren, *The Purpose Driven Life* (Grand Rapids, Michigan: Zondervan, 2002), 19.

2 Stephen R. Covey, *The 7 Habits of Highly Effective People* (New York, New York: Simon & Schuster, 1994), 140.

3 Howard Schultz, *From the Ground Up* (New York, New York: Random House, 2019), 8.

4 Howard Schultz, *Pour Your Heart Into It* (New York, New York: Hyperion, 1997), 4.

5 Ibid., 13.

6 Ibid., 15-16.

7 Howard Schultz, *From the Ground Up* (New York, New York: Random House, 2019), 168.

8 Howard Schultz, *Pour Your Heart Into It* (New York, New York: Hyperion, 1997), 25.

9 Ibid., 26-27.

10 Ibid., 29.

11 Ibid., 34.

12 Ibid., 52-53.

13 Ibid., 69.

14 Ibid., 12.

15 Howard Schultz, *From the Ground Up* (New York, New York: Random House, 2019), 26.

16 Howard Schultz, *Pour Your Heart Into It* (New York, New York: Hyperion, 1997), 105-106

17 Howard Schultz, *From the Ground Up* (New York, New York: Random House, 2019), 28.

18 Ibid., 46.

19 Ibid., 46.

20 Ibid., 46.

21 Ibid., 47-48.

22 Ibid., 80.

23 Ibid., 94.

24 Howard Schultz, *From the Ground Up* (New York, New York: Random House, 2019), 178.

25 Ibid., 215.

26 Bruce Springsteen, *Born To Run* (New York, New York: Simon & Schuster, 2016), 9.

27 Ibid., 16.

28 Ibid., 42

29 Ibid., 43.

30 Ibid., 49.

31 Ibid., 50-51.

32 Ibid., 64.

33 Ibid., 66.

34 Ibid., 72.

35 Ibid., 73.

36 Ibid., 89-90.

37 Ibid., 92.

38 Ibid., 95.

39 Ibid., 97.

40 Ibid., 98.

41   Ibid., 106-107.
42   Ibid., 117.
43   Ibid., 137-138.
44   Ibid., 145.
45   Ibid., 149-150.
46   Ibid., 186.
47   Ibid., 183.
48   Ibid., 193.
49   Ibid., 222.
50   Ibid., 225.
51   Ibid., 233.
52   Ibid., 276.
53   Ibid., 281.
54   Ibid., 283, 285.
55   Ibid., 186-187.
56   Ibid., 283-285.
57   Ibid., 309.
58   Ibid., 309.
59   Ibid., 311-312.
60   Doris Kearns Goodwin, *The Bully Pulpit* (New York, New York: Simon & Schuster, 2013), 67-68.
61   Ibid., 71.
62   Ibid., 72.
63   Ibid., 74.
64   Ibid., 74.
65   Ibid., 76.
66   Ibid., 77.
67   Ibid., 77.
68   Ibid., 78.
69   Ibid., 78.
70   Ibid., 130.

71 Ibid., 206.
72 Ibid., 206.
73 Ibid. 207.
74 Ibid., 209.
75 Ibid., 244.
76 Ibid., 246.
77 Ibid., 283.
78 Ibid., 246.
79 Ibid., 247.
80 Ibid., 253.
81 Ibid., 300.
82 Ibid., 402.
83 Ibid., 254.
84 Ibid., 254.
85 Ibid., 254-255.
86 Ibid., 292.
87 Ibid., 295.
88 Ibid., 297.
89 Ibid., 299.
90 Ibid., 299-300.
91 Ibid., 342.
92 Ibid., 343.
93 Ibid., 400.
94 Ibid., 437.
95 Ibid., 440.
96 Ibid., 440-441.
97 Ibid., 442-443.
98 Ibid., 462-463.
99 Ibid., 214.
100 Rick Warren, *The Purpose Driven Life* (Grand Rapids, Michigan: Zondervan, 2002), 234-235.

101 Ibid., 194.

102 Lewis B. Smedes, *The Art of Forgiving* (New York, New York: Random House, 1996), xii-xiii.

103 Lewis B. Smedes, *Forgive & Forget; Healing the Hurts We Don't Deserve* (New York, New York: HarperCollins Publishers, 1984), 94.

104 Rick Warren, *The Purpose Driven Life* (Grand Rapids, Michigan: Zondervan, 2002), 241.

105 Bill Hybels, *Too Busy Not to Pray* (Downers Grove, Illinois: InterVarsity Press, 1998), 164.

106 Henry T. Blackaby & Claude V. King, *Experiencing God* (Nashville, Tennessee: LifeWay Press, 1990) 147.

107 Marcus J. Borg, *Jesus A New Vision* (San Francisco, California: Harper & Row, 1987) 192-193.

108 Bruce Wilkinson, *Secrets of the Vine* (Sisters, Oregon: Multnomah, Inc. 2001) 117-118.

109 C. Bernard Ruffin, *The Twelve, The Lives of the Apostles After Calvary* (Huntington, Indiana: Our Sunday Visitor, Inc., 1997), 33.

110 Ibid., 50.

111 Ibid., 51-53

112 Ibid., 54.

113 William Steuart McBirnie, *The Search for the Twelve Apostles* (Wheaton, Illinois: Tyndale House Publishers, 1973) 65-66

114 N.T. Wright, *Paul* (New York, New York: HarperOne, 2018), 11.

115 Ibid., 79.

116 Ibid., 74.

117 Ibid., 10.

118 Ibid., 21-22.

119 Ibid., 15.

120 Ibid., 15-16.

121 Ibid., 4.

122 Sam Hunter, *The Missing Link* (Houston, Texas: High Bridge Books, 2019), 245.

123 N.T. Wright, *Paul* (New York, New York: HarperOne, 2018), 386.

124 Ibid., 386.

125 J. Lee Grady, *10 Lies the Church Tells Women* (Lake Mary, Florida: Charisma House, 2000), 51-52.

126 Rick Warren, *The Purpose Driven Life* (Grand Rapids, Michigan: Zondervan, 2002), 32.

127 John C. Maxwell, *Failing Forward* (Nashville, Tennessee: THOMAS Nelson Publishers, 2007), 182.

128 Howard Schultz, *Pour Your Heart Into It* (New York, New York: Hyperion, 1997), 274.

129 Bruce Springsteen, *Born To Run* (New York, New York: Simon & Schuster, 2016), 278.

130 Howard Schultz, *Pour Your Heart Into It* (New York, New York: Hyperion, 1997), 44.

131 Sam Hunter, *The Missing Link* (Houston, Texas: High Bridge Books, 2019), 31-32.